International Labour and Employment Compliance Handbook

www.kluwerlawonline.com

Labour and Employment Compliance in the United States

International Bar Association

Labour and Employment Compliance in the United States

Ninth Edition

Andrew J. Boling
Robert J. Mignin
Madeline F. Kelleher
David M. Serwer

This publication is part of the International Labour and Employment Compliance Handbook, available on www.kluwerlawonline.com

Editors: Salvador del Rey and Robert J. Mignin
Associate Editor: Juan Bonilla

the global voice of the legal profession

Wolters Kluwer

Published by:
Kluwer Law International B.V.
PO Box 316
2400 AH Alphen aan den Rijn
The Netherlands
E-mail: lrs-sales@wolterskluwer.com
Website: www.wolterskluwer.com/en/solutions/kluwerlawinternational

Sold and distributed by:
Wolters Kluwer Legal & Regulatory U.S.
920 Links Avenue
Landisville, PA 17538
United States of America
E-mail: customer.service@wolterskluwer.com

ISBN 978-94-035-0189-5

e-Book: ISBN 978-94-035-0199-4
web-PDF: ISBN 978-94-035-0209-0

All listed titles are also available on lrus.wolterskluwer.com

1. Argentina: Julio César Stefanoni Zani & Enrique Alfredo Betemps, *Labour and Employment Compliance in Argentina, 12th edition*, 2024 (ISBN 978-94-035-4878-4)
2. Australia: John Tuck, Stephen Price, Rosemary Roach, Jack de Flamingh, Nicholas Ellery & Nick Le Mare, *Labour and Employment Compliance in Australia, 6th edition*, 2021 (ISBN 978-94-035-3914-0)
3. Belgium: Chris Van Olmen, *Labour and Employment Compliance in Belgium, 9th edition*, 2024 (ISBN 978-94-035-0089-8)
4. Brazil: Rodrigo Seizo Takano, Andrea Giamondo Massei & Murilo Caldeira Germiniani, *Labour and Employment Compliance in Brazil, 11th edition*, 2024 (ISBN 978-94-035-4938-5)
5. Canada: Kevin Coon, *Labour and Employment Compliance in Canada, 3rd edition*, 2023 (ISBN 978-90-411-9339-1)
6. Chile: Gerardo Otero A., María Dolores Echeverría F., María Ignacia Romero A., Juan Pablo Cortés R. & Javier Sabido, *Labour and Employment Compliance in Chile, 12th edition*, 2024 (ISBN 978-94-035-4968-2)
7. China: King & Wood Mallesons, *Labour and Employment Compliance in China, 6th edition*, 2021 (ISBN 978-94-035-3894-5)
8. France: Pascale Lagesse, *Labour and Employment Compliance in France, 12th edition*, 2024 (ISBN 978-94-035-0219-9)
9. Germany: Gerlind Wisskirchen & Martin Lützeler, *Labour and Employment Compliance in Germany, 11th edition*, 2023 (ISBN 978-94-035-2347-7)
10. India: Manishi Pathak, *Labour and Employment Compliance in India, 12th edition*, 2024 (ISBN 978-94-035-4908-8)
11. Ireland: Duncan Inverarity & Tríona Sugrue, *Labour and Employment Compliance in Ireland, 10th edition*, 2023 (ISBN 978-94-035-2227-2)
12. Israel: Pnina Broder-Manor & Ilan Winder, *Labour and Employment Compliance in Israel, 11th edition*, 2024 (ISBN 978-94-035-0099-7)
13. Italy: Angelo Zambelli, *Labour and Employment Compliance in Italy, 12th edition*, 2024 (ISBN 978-94-035-0009-6)
14. Japan: Yoshikazu Sugino, *Labour and Employment Compliance in Japan, 12th edition*, 2024 (ISBN 978-94-035-3158-8)
15. Republic of Korea: Sang Wook Cho, Soojung Lee, Christopher Mandel & Tae Eun Lee, *Labour and Employment Compliance in the Republic of Korea, 9th edition*, 2023 (ISBN 978-94-035-2167-1)
16. Mexico: Oscar De La Vega Gómez, *Labour and Employment Compliance in Mexico, 11th edition*, 2023 (ISBN 978-94-035-2377-4)
17. The Netherlands: Els de Wind & Cara Pronk, *Labour and Employment Compliance in the Netherlands, 5th edition*, 2022 (ISBN 978-94-035-1594-6)
18. Poland: Barbara Jóźwik, *Labour and Employment Compliance in Poland, 11th edition*, 2023 (ISBN 978-94-035-2407-8)
19. Russia: Anna-Stefaniya Chepik, *Labour and Employment Compliance in Russia*, 2013 (ISBN 978-90-411-4925-1)
20. Saudi Arabia: Sara Khoja & Sarit Thomas, *Labour and Employment Compliance in Saudi Arabia, 7th edition*, 2024 (ISBN 978-94-035-0129-1)

21. South Africa: Susan Stelzner†, Stuart Harrison, Brian Patterson & Zahida Ebrahim, *Labour and Employment Compliance in South Africa, 11th edition*, 2023 (ISBN 978-94-035-2257-9)
22. Spain: Salvador del Rey & Ana Campos, *Labour and Employment Compliance in Spain, 12th edition*, 2024 (978-94-035-0039-3)
23. Turkey: Elif Nur Çakır Vurgun, Gökhan Akçaalan, Özgür Kızıltan & Zeynep Adıyaman, *Labour and Employment Compliance in Turkey, 9th edition*, 2023 (ISBN 978-94-035-2287-6)
24. United Arab Emirates: Sara Khoja & Sarit Thomas, *Labour and Employment Compliance in the United Arab Emirates, 11th edition*, 2024 (ISBN 978-94-035-0159-8)
25. United Kingdom: Ed Mills, Ailie Murray, Anna West, Gareth Walls & Olivia Boyle, *Labour and Employment Compliance in The United Kingdom, 4th edition*, 2023 (ISBN 978-94-035-2317-0)
26. United States: Andrew J. Boling, Robert J. Mignin, Madeline F. Kelleher & David M. Serwer, *Labour and Employment Compliance in the United States, 9th edition*, 2024 (ISBN 978-94-035-0189-5)

International Bar Association
The Global Voice of the Legal Profession

The International Bar Association (IBA), established in 1947, is the world's leading organization of international legal practitioners, bar associations and law societies. The IBA influences the development of international law reform and shapes the future of the legal profession throughout the world. It has a membership of over 40,000 individual lawyers and almost 200 bar associations and law societies spanning all continents. It has considerable expertise in providing assistance to the global legal community.

Grouped into two divisions – the Legal Practice Division and the Public and Professional Interest Division – the IBA covers all practice areas and professional interests, providing members with access to leading experts and up-to-date information. Through the various committees of the divisions, the IBA enables an interchange of information and views among its members as to laws, practices and professional responsibilities relating to the practice of business law around the globe. Additionally, the IBA's high-quality publications and world-class conferences provide unrivalled professional development and network-building opportunities for international legal practitioners and professional associates.

The IBA's Bar Issues Commission provides an invaluable forum for IBA member organisations to discuss all matters relating to law at an international level.

The IBA's Human Rights Institute (IBAHRI) works across the Association, to promote, protect and enforce human rights under a just rule of law, and to preserve the independence of the judiciary and the legal profession worldwide.

Other institutions established by the IBA include the Southern Africa Litigation Centre and the International Legal Assistance Consortium.

Employment and Industrial Relations Law Committee

The aims of the committee are to develop and exchange knowledge of employment and industrial relations law and practice. Members support each other through the provision of innovative ideas and practical assistance on day-to-day issues. In addition, through its journal and through presentations, conferences, the committee ensures the dissemination of up-to-date law and practice in this highly important business area.

International Bar Association Global Employment Institute

The IBA Global Employment Institute (IBA GEI) was formed in early 2010 for the purpose of developing for multinationals and worldwide institutions a global and strategic approach to the key legal issues in the human resources and human capital fields.

Drawing on the resources and expertise of the IBA membership, the IBA GEI will provide a unique contribution in the field of employment, discrimination and immigration law, on a diverse range of global issues, to private and public organizations throughout the world. The IBA GEI is designed to enhance the management, performance and productivity of these organizations and help achieve best practice in their human capital and management functions from a strategic perspective.

The IBA GEI will become the leading voice and authority on global HR issues by virtue of having a number of the world's leading labour and employment practitioners in its ranks, and the support and resource of the world's largest association of international lawyers.

Further information

International Bar Association, 4th Floor, 10 St Bride Street, London EC4A 4AD, United Kingdom, Tel: +44 (0)20 7842 0090, Fax: +44 (0)20 7842 0091, E-mail: member@int-bar.org, www.ibanet.org

About the International Labour and Employment Compliance Handbook

From 1976 through 1988, the International Bar Association and Kluwer Law International published the groundbreaking International Handbook on Contracts of Employment. This Handbook provided one of the first global overviews of the law of the international employment relationship.

Since publishing the first edition, globalization of business has created an increased demand for knowledge of labor and employment laws throughout the world. Therefore, along with Kluwer, we decided to publish an updated Handbook which we have titled the International Labour and Employment Compliance Handbook.

This new Handbook was intended to be a practical guide by providing a general overview of key labor and employment issues in multiple jurisdictions. Each chapter was written so that it is easy to understand by lawyers and non-lawyers alike. Each country author has also followed a standard outline to assist readers in analysing employment issues in each country.

The first edition of this new Handbook included nineteen (19) different countries.

This Handbook would not have been possible without the help and assistance of many people. Most importantly, the individual country authors are all distinguished legal practitioners who spent considerable time drafting and revising their country reports to meet difficult deadlines. We thank each of them. Our friends at Kluwer, especially Ewa Szkatula, have done a wonderful job in keeping the editors and the authors on schedule. Finally, we want to also express our gratitude to Cuatrecasas, Gonçalves Pereira, and Baker & McKenzie LLP for their valuable assistance in the coordination and organization of this project. Our warmest thanks to each of them.

Because of the success of the Handbook,Wolters Kluwer Law & Business decided to publish each country report also as a separate book to give a choice in obtaining the information. We hope this new format will be a helpful and useful resource just like the Handbook. Both formats are available in print and online.

The Editors

Salvador del Rey Guanter
Robert J. Mignin

March 2013

Table of Contents

United States

AUTHORS

Andrew J. Boling

Andrew J. Boling is a retired partner in the Chicago office of Baker & McKenzie and is currently the Employment Chair of Kelleher + Holland, LLC. Mr. Boling represents employers in a variety of cross-border and domestic employment law matters. Mr. Boling also counsels and represents employers and management in all types of U.S. employment and labor matters. He has represented companies in hundreds of lawsuits and administrative proceedings throughout the United States (U.S.). Mr. Boling has written and lectured extensively on employment law issues, and most recently on the extraterritorial application of U.S. employment laws, data protection laws and employee privacy, enforcement of restricted covenants and cross-border employment agreements. Mr. Boling has been recognized as a Leading Lawyer in the Legal 500, by Acritas as a Client Service All-Star and by *Euromoney* as one of the thirty *Best of the Best* employment lawyers in the U.S.

Madeline F. Kelleher

Madeline F. Kelleher is an attorney in the Employment and Corporate Groups at Kelleher + Holland, LLC. Ms. Kelleher specializes in the representation and counseling of employers, management, and senior executives during all stages of the employment relationship as well as in relation to business formations and mergers and acquisitions. She represents her clients in cases dealing with a variety of employment-related matters, including executive contracts and compensation, hiring and terminating employees, restrictive covenants and trade secret protection, defense of employment claims, and general employment counseling. Ms. Kelleher has been recognized nationally by Best Lawyers®, receiving its Ones to Watch® award for the years of 2023 and 2024. She is also on the Illinois board of Midwest Business Brokers and Intermediaries (MBBI©) and has also been recognized as one of MBBI's Rising Stars for the years of 2023 and 2024.

Robert J. Mignin

Robert J. Mignin was a retired partner in the Chicago office of Baker & McKenzie LLP and passed away in the fall of 2023. Mr. Mignin specialized in employment and labor relations matters, as well as matters involving protection of a company's confidential business information, noncompete agreements, technology, executive employment agreements, and investigation of harassment and discrimination complaints. He also represented employers in mediation and arbitration of discrimination and harassment claims and all related employment litigation (single plaintiff and class action) in federal and state courts. Mr. Mignin also counseled and advised clients on the development of corporate policies and complaint procedures, workplace and corporate compliance programs, and all employment and labor issues arising in the context of any domestic or international restructuring, merger, acquisition and/or sale of a business or assets.

David M. Serwer is a Partner at Baker & Hostetler LLP in Chicago, Illinois, and is the firm's Immigration Practice Lead. He advises, represents, supports, and manages corporate business immigration client engagements and relationships in a wide range of industries, including IT, healthcare, manufacturing, engineering, and financial. He has intensive experience practicing exclusively in employment-based immigration law and counsels HR, Legal and Executive teams on immigration-related corporate compliance matters and M&A strategies from startups to Fortune 100 multinational companies.

Messrs Boling and Mignin wish to acknowledge their former partners at Baker & McKenzie, LLP—William Dugan (labor and employment), Brian Hengesbaugh, Amy de la Lama (privacy), Christopher Guldberg (employee benefits and taxation), John M. Murphy (trade secrets) and Ginger Partee (immigration)—for their material and helpful contributions to prior editions of this chapter.

Finally, this update is dedicated to the memory of Robert Mignin. He was a lawyer's lawyer, an inspiring mentor to countless attorneys, and a dear friend.

Legal Compliance with Employment, Labor, Benefits, Compensation and Immigration Laws and Regulations

1. LEGAL FRAMEWORK: EMPLOYMENT LAWS

The hallmark principle of employment law in the United States (U.S.) is "employment at-will." This means that either party to the employment relationship—employee or employer—may end (terminate) the employment relationship at any time with or without prior notice for any reason or no reason at all. Importantly, in the U.S., there is no "contractual" right to employment.

The employment "at-will" principle in the U.S. is subject to several exceptions. For example, even though an employer is permitted to end the employment relationship for any or no reason, an employer cannot take any action based on an employee's disability, race, gender, age, national origin, religion, color, genetic information, pregnancy, veteran status, sexual orientation or other state, local, or federally protected characteristics.

Federal employment and labor laws apply to most employees working in the private sector in the U.S. In addition, state and local laws and regulations provide rights to employees that may be the same or exceed those granted by federal law. Accordingly, the laws of the state, county or city where the employee works should always be consulted with respect to any employment-related issue.

2. CONTRACTS OF EMPLOYMENT

2.1. Overview

In general, private sector employees in the U.S. have relatively limited employment rights compared to most other countries. Under the "at-will" employment doctrine, an employer in the U.S. is generally free to terminate an employee for any reason at any time with or without notice. In addition, other than laws relating to advance notice in mass layoff or plant shutdown situations, or possible obligations under union contracts, there is no obligation for an employer to provide terminated employees with any notice of termination or any severance pay or benefits.

2.2. Written Employment Contracts

A significant exception to the "at-will" employment doctrine is a written employment contract which establishes an employer's obligations and employee's rights during and upon termination of the employment agreement. The vast majority of employees in the U.S., however, are *not* covered by an employment contract. Written employment contracts are generally provided only to executives, professionals or highly technical or other specialized employees.

2.2.1. Employment Contracts

If an employer enters into a written employment contract with an employee, the term of such contract is often for a set period of time. It is possible, however, to have an open-ended contract, which provides for termination upon reasonable notice given by either party. As a general rule, written employment contracts allow for termination only for "cause" as defined by the contract. Written employment contracts also establish compensation and benefits for the employee during the term of the contract and often provide for the payment of certain severance and other post-termination commitments. It is possible to have an employment contract while expressly preserving the employer's termination rights under the employment-at-will doctrine.

2.2.2. Collective Bargaining Agreements

Less than 10% of employees in the U.S. private sector belong to a union or are covered by a labor contract. Labor contracts set wages, benefits and working conditions for employees for a set period of time and often establish rules which must be followed before a company can discipline or terminate an employee. Most collective bargaining agreements also establish a dispute resolution process which includes grievances and final and binding labor arbitration.

2.3. Oral Contracts

Binding employment contracts can sometimes also be created by verbal statements to an employee by a manager or supervisor or other company representatives. For example, a manager who states to an employee that "you will have a job with us as long as your work is good" may have created a contract of employment. In some states, an oral contract could prohibit termination of an employee except for "cause" and remove a worker from the application of the "at-will" employment rule.

Employers can also be contractually bound to employees under the theory of promissory estoppel. Courts may use this doctrine to enforce oral promises if an employer made a clear oral promise upon which the employee relied to his or her detriment.

The following examples of statements made by a manager to an employee may constitute an enforceable oral contractual promise in the U.S.: (i) "I will give you a pay raise if you continue doing your job;" (ii) "The company wants you to have job security and you will always have a job;" (iii) "You will always have a job as long as I am with the company;" and (iv) "We have a no lay off policy."

2.4. Employee Handbooks

There is no legal obligation in the U.S. for employers to have any written handbooks, policies or procedures. Most companies, however, provide employees with some type of a handbook or other written policies which set forth and describe terms and conditions of employment. Courts in several states have held that the wording in handbooks or policy manuals can create a binding employment contract sufficient to erode the "at-will" employment status.

Statements in handbooks or policy manuals that might create an employment contract include: (i) "All employees will be given a written warning before termination;" (ii) "Employees will only be terminated for the reasons set forth in our work rules;" (iii) "Employees can be terminated for any reason during the probationary period."

To reduce the risk that written employee handbooks or policy manuals could rise to the level of contractual promises, employers in the U.S. are advised to include in any written policies or handbooks the following type of statement:

> The contents of this [policy/handbook] are presented as a matter of information to guide you in your employment and are not promises or guarantees of employment. The [company] reserves the right to modify, revoke, suspend, terminate or change at its sole discretion any or all

policies or procedures or benefit plans in whole or in part, at any time, with or without notice. The language used in this [policy/handbook] and in [our] policies is not intended to create, nor is it to be construed as a contract (express or implied) between the [company] and any employee or group of employees.

Your employment with the [company] is "at-will," meaning that you or the [company] may terminate your employment at any time for any reason, with or without notice. Nothing in the [handbook] or our policies is intended to change or alter your status as an employee "at-will." Your employment "at-will" can be changed only by a written authorization signed by the [President].

2.5. Job Descriptions

Although not legally required in most circumstances, written job descriptions can also create an employment contract or other enforceable promises. To prevent a job description from becoming a contract, specific disclaimers should be inserted in job descriptions, similar to the statement set forth in section 2.4 above.

2.6. Offer Letters

There is also no legal obligation in the U.S. for companies to provide a candidate with a written job offer. Nevertheless, most employers in the U.S. provide some type of offer letters to prospective employees. The offer letter should generally provide a description of the employee's new job, reporting responsibilities, compensation package and address eligibility to work under federal immigration law. Offer letters should also state that the employee is being hired "at-will" and that the final hiring decision will be subject to applicable background screens, preemployment tests and employment verifications.

2.7. Checklist

To maintain the "at-will" employment status with employees, employers in the U.S. should always remember the following:

- Handbooks and policy and procedure manuals should *not* contain any promise or guarantee that would erode the "at-will" nature of the employment relationship or create an employment contract.

- Employment applications, offer letters and job descriptions should not make any statements which are inconsistent with the employment "at-will" relationship and should include a "disclaimer" as described in section 2.4.
- Every manager, supervisor or HR representative involved in the hiring process should be trained to avoid making any statements which could create a promise and undermine the "at-will" relationship.

3. RECRUITING, INTERVIEWING, SCREENING AND HIRING EMPLOYEES

3.1. Overview

Hiring and retaining qualified and skilled employees is one of the biggest challenges facing employers in the U.S. The threat of legal liability for poor recruiting, negligent hiring, discrimination claims, or wrongful termination requires employers to make careful hiring decisions.

3.2. Recruiting

When a company is first looking to fill a job, it is always advisable to create a job description which describes only essential and nonessential duties of the job. The job description should not contain references to physical or mental disabilities or any other protected characteristics. Additionally, employers using artificial intelligence (AI) tools for screening candidates or employees for employment decisions should be aware of state and local governments laws prohibiting usage and ensure the AI-based decision-making tools do not screen candidates based upon protected characteristics (*see* section 22.11). The employer should list the job opening through a variety of different external sources to solicit as many skilled and diverse applicants as possible. Employers should also refer to their state's job posting requirements to ensure compliance. For example, a growing number of states and local governments have enacted pay transparency laws, requiring employers to include the salary or wage range they plan to pay an employee when advertising an open employment position.

3.3. Employment Applications

Employment applications are helpful for selecting the best employees. All of the questions on an employment application should be job related. Different jobs may require different applications or different questions.

The following can be stated in a job application: (i) questions about educational background; (ii) questions about past work experience; (iii) a statement that the application is not an employment offer or a contract; (iv) a statement that employment is "at-will"; and (v) a statement that all questions must be truthfully answered and any false answers will result in the applicant not being hired or possibly terminated.

The following should *not* be included in a job application: (i) questions about the applicant's medical history; and (ii) any questions about the applicant's sex, age, religion, disability, national origin, race, color, genetic information, marital status, height or weight, physical or mental condition, sexual preference, race or other protected characteristics. Importantly, questions about the applicant's past salary or compensation history are now prohibited under some state and local laws.

Only information that is necessary to determine if a person has the skills and is qualified for a particular job should be asked on an employment application.

Employment applications should also state that employment is "at-will" and alert the applicant that any offer of employment will be subject to the company's policies and procedures.

3.4. Preemployment Process

As a general rule, employers in the U.S. should only ask questions relating to an applicant's ability to perform a particular job. For example, an employer may ask whether an applicant can perform the physical requirements of the job and if the applicant can satisfy these requirements or perform certain job tasks. An employer may also ask whether a candidate can perform the duties of the job "with or without reasonable accommodation." An employer may also ask about an applicant's non-medical qualifications and skills, such as the applicant's education, prior work history and any special skills and licenses.

3.5. Preemployment Tests and Examinations

An employer may require applicants to take preemployment tests to determine if the applicant has the necessary skills, abilities and job-related knowledge to carry out the duties of the position—but only if the tests do not disproportionately screen out for no job-related reason any persons in a protected group. As a matter of best practice, preemployment tests should be validated to establish that they are not discriminating against protected individuals.

An employer in the U.S. may require an applicant to take a job-related medical examination but only *after* an applicant has been offered employment. In most states, an employer may also require an applicant to take a drug or alcohol test as a condition of employment.

3.6. Background, Reference and Credit Checks

As a general rule, a company in the U.S. may ask about an applicant's past job and education history and request business and personal references. Additionally, subject to state and local law requirements, an employer may ask questions about an applicant's criminal background if the inquiry is limited to criminal convictions, although given the increased hostility to such inquiries at the state and local level, it is best to reserve this inquiry where criminal history is directly related to the job position at hand. Questions about arrest records should *never* be asked of an applicant. Several states have also restricted the use of credit history. Employers should only ask about an applicant's credit history if the job would give the employee access to company money or funds. The Fair Credit Reporting Act (FCRA) requires notification to the applicant if a third-party company is used to research or obtain information about an applicant's credit or background information. The Equal Employment Opportunity Commission (EEOC) will closely scrutinize the job-relatedness of any background checks or tests used to screen candidates, particularly if such checks or tests disproportionately exclude applicants in protected categories.

3.7. Interviewing

Most companies conduct in-person interviews with an applicant after initial screenings by HR. Interviews allow the company to ascertain the applicant's ability to perform a job duty and discuss his or her skills and background and references.

Employers should train all persons involved in the interview process to avoid asking any questions that are related to an applicant's sex, gender identity, disability, age, religion, race, color, national origin, genetic information, sexual orientation, parental or marital status or other protected status. By providing all persons in the interview process a current job description of the position as well as objective qualifications and other screening criteria, an employer can avoid unintentional discrimination.

The following topics may be discussed during an interview: (i) attendance and reliability; (ii) education background; (iii) prior job experience and performance; (iv) technical and other special skills; (v) expectations and attitude; (vi) ability to learn and problem solve; and (vii) career goals.

3.8. Hiring Procedures

During the hiring process, an employer should only make statements about the nature of the job and the candidate's intended duties and responsibilities. An employer may explain any applicable policies and procedures pertaining to employment. An employer may also explain salary and any other benefits and tell the applicant that any job offer will be subject to the applicant successfully passing any preemployment tests or examinations.

3.9. Fines and Penalties

An applicant who is denied employment for unlawful reasons may file a claim of discrimination with a state or federal agency. The applicant may also file a lawsuit in federal or state court. An applicant unlawfully denied employment could recover attorney's fees, as well as actual, compensatory and punitive damages as a result of the employer's failure to hire him or her.

3.10. Checklist of Dos and Don'ts

- Applicants should complete all portions of an application.
- An employer should develop current job descriptions.
- All persons involved in the interview, screening and hiring process should be trained to ask only job-related questions.
- Background checks and tests may be conducted of all applicants before making a final offer of employment.
- Employers should never make any promises of permanent employment.

4. MANAGING PERFORMANCE/CONDUCT

4.1. Overview

Although not legally required in the U.S., performance evaluations of current employees are often important in the employment process. An employer should use job evaluations as a tool to keep employees informed of their individual job performance. Performance evaluations can often be used as evidence in employment litigation. For example, if a recent performance evaluation of an employee is positive, it is difficult to argue the employee was actually a poor performer even though the employee may have been underperforming. Performance evaluations should always be completed as honestly as possible and reviewed with the employee on a regular basis.

An employer should conduct performance evaluations for all employees. A good performance evaluation should describe both the employee's strengths and weaknesses.

4.2. Coaching and Counseling

Although not legally required in the U.S., supervisors can and should coach and counsel employees by familiarizing them with the duties and responsibilities of their job and suggesting areas of performance that might need improvement.

4.3. Written Evaluations

Employers should complete some type of annual written performance evaluations for each employee. Employers should avoid evaluating employees based on specific personality traits. Written evaluations should analyze job-specific behavior and skills. Companies should train supervisors and managers on how to properly prepare written performance evaluations. An employer should avoid using any evaluations which could be viewed as a personal attack on the employee.

4.4. Warnings and Suspensions

The employment "at-will" doctrine gives companies in the U.S. the discretion to terminate employees without warning or any advance notice. The majority of employers in the U.S., however, follow some type of progressive discipline process. After an employee receives coaching or counseling, an employer should prepare a formal record of the employee's poor job performance or conduct. Employers should also document in writing a "last chance" warning as well as suspension prior to termination. A last chance warning or suspension gives the employee sufficient notice that his or her job performance is unacceptable and that he or she will be subject to more serious discipline, and possibly termination, if performance does not improve. In the case of severe misconduct or underperformance, a prior warning is not necessary.

4.5. CHECKLIST

- Performance evaluations and disciplinary warnings should be reviewed with the employee on a regular basis so that he or she has an opportunity to improve his or her behavior.
- Performance evaluations should be based on job-related factors and skills rather than personal traits.
- Employees should be told if they are doing a good job and also told about any performance weaknesses. A performance improvement process should set timelines for the employee.
- Managers and supervisors should be honest, candid and respectful when discussing an employee's work performance.

5. TERMINATION OF EMPLOYEES FOR PERFORMANCE OR DISCIPLINARY REASONS

5.1. OVERVIEW

"At-will" employment is the general rule in the U.S. Federal and state laws and court decisions have made some "exceptions" that restrict an employer's ability to discharge or discipline employees "at-will."

Common "exceptions" to the at-will doctrine include: (i) a written employment contract or a collective bargaining agreement with a "cause" termination provision; (ii) termination for any reason contrary to public policy, such as filing a workers' compensation claim, or engaging in other protected behavior; and (iii) any discipline or termination which is based on the employee's race, national origin, ethnicity, age, gender, religion, marital status, sexual orientation, union activity, disability or any other protected status. One state, Montana, requires "good cause" to terminate an employee after the employee has satisfied a probationary period.

In addition to claims under federal or state statutes, employees may also file lawsuits in a state or federal court challenging termination decisions for several reasons: (i) intentional infliction of emotional distress (these are claims based on the manner by which the employee was discharged); (ii) tortious interference with contractual relationships (these are claims that arise when an employee alleges that another employee communicated false information that resulted in the employee's termination); (iii) fraud and negligent misrepresentation (these are claims that arise when a former employee alleges that false statements were made about his or her past employment); (iv) defamation (these are claims by an employee that allege managers or supervisors made false statements that injured his or her reputation); and (v) invasion of privacy (these are claims based on allegations that a company violated the employee's right to privacy, such as searching an employee's belongings or inquiring about an employee's personal life).

Even an employee who *voluntarily* quits his or her job may still bring a claim against a former employer for "constructive discharge." Under this theory, a former employee can allege that the employer created a working environment that was so intolerable or hostile that a reasonable person would have quit his or her employment. These claims commonly arise in situations where an employee raises allegations of sexual or racial harassment or retaliation in the workplace.

5.2. Separation/Severance Pay

Private sector employers in the U.S. are generally not required by law to pay any severance or separation pay to a terminated employee regardless of the length of time the employee worked for the company.

Employers who elect to provide terminated employees with some type of separation or severance pay or benefits should consider the following: (i) other terminated employees will expect the same treatment; (ii) any severance or separation pay policy should state that an employee must execute a general release of all potential claims and a covenant not to sue to be eligible for such pay; and (iii) federal age discrimination laws require that terminated employees over the age of 40 be given the option to review any release of potential age claims for twenty-one days and have the option to revoke the agreement seven days after signing. Employees over the age of 40 also have forty-five days to consider the release if they are terminated as part of a larger group. In such circumstances, they are entitled to information relating to the selection criteria used for the group and the ages of those employees selected for termination. Employers offering severance agreements with confidentiality and nondisparagement provisions to employees covered under section 7 of the National Labor Relations Act (NLRA) should be aware of the National Labor Relations Board (NLRB)'s recent decision in *McLaren Macomb*, which held that it is an unfair labor practice under the NLRA for employers to offer, or even merely proffer, employees severance agreements that contain overly broad nondisparagement and confidentiality clauses that have a reasonable tendency to interfere with, restrain, or coerce employees in the exercise of their NLRA section 7 rights. In light of this decision, employers in the U.S. are advised consider supplementing any restrictive covenants in severance agreements that could violate an employee's section 7 rights with disclaimers confirming the provisions are not intended to restrict an employee (or former employee) from exercising their section 7 rights under the NLRA, including filing a Charge with or speaking to the NLRB. For example, the following type of statement could be included as a disclaimer for a nondisparagement provision:

> The Parties agree that nothing in this agreement prevents [Employee] from discussing or disclosing information about the unlawful acts or any conduct [Employee] has reason to believe is unlawful in the workplace. In addition, nothing in this agreement prevents [Employee] from participating in Section 7 activities under the National Labor Relations Act.

Likewise, for example, the following type of statement could be included as a disclaimer for a generally applicable confidentiality provision, subject to various state law requirements:

> The Parties agree that this confidentiality provision is not intended to waive any claims or rights that cannot be waived as a matter of law. Nothing herein prohibits [Employee] from filing a charge with or participating in any investigation undertaken by a government agency, except that [Employee] hereby waives any rights to recover any money in connection with such a charge or investigation with respect to released claims, whether filed by [Employee] or on [Employee]'s behalf by another person or entity.

5.3. Fines and Penalties

A terminated employee may file a lawsuit against his or her former employer in a state or federal court or file charges with federal, state or local administrative agencies alleging that the termination was a violation of discrimination laws or common law. If the employee prevails in a lawsuit, the employee may recover back pay, future pay, compensatory damages, attorneys' fees and punitive damages.

5.4. Checklist

- All employees should be treated fairly and subject to the same terms and conditions of employment regardless of their race, sex, religion, age, disability, sexual orientation or other protected status.
- As a general rule, employees should first be counseled and given the opportunity to improve their job performance before discipline or termination.

- The types of behavior or gross misconduct that could result in immediate termination—before progressive discipline—should be stated in a policy manual or handbook.

6. LAYOFFS, REDUCTIONS IN FORCE AND/OR REDUNDANCIES AS A RESULT OF JOB ELIMINATIONS OR OTHER RESTRUCTURING

6.1. Overview

There are relatively few restrictions imposed on private sector employers in the U.S. who want to eliminate jobs, shut down facilities, reduce working hours or terminate or lay off employees. The only exceptions would involve employees who are covered by an employment agreement or a collective bargaining agreement. Those agreements may specify procedures that must be followed before implementing a layoff or other forms of workforce reduction or termination of employment.

6.2. Reductions in Force/Layoffs/Job Eliminations

The federal Worker Adjustment and Retraining Notification Act (WARN) requires companies to provide advance notice under some circumstances to employees prior to a layoff or plant shutdown so that the employees can begin to search for other employment. The WARN Act requires employers to give advance notice to unions, nonunion employees and certain government officials sixty days prior to a mass layoff or plant closing. An employer must give written notice to the union representatives, employees without representation, local government officials and the state dislocated worker unit.

WARN applies to private employers in the U.S. with 100 or more full-time employees (not including employees who have less than six months on the job and workers who work fewer than twenty hours per week); or 100 or more employees (full and part-time) who, in total, work at least 4,000 hours per week, not including overtime (workers at different sites are combined to determine whether the business meets the 100 employee threshold). The WARN Act establishes minimum coverage. Some states have enacted more stringent requirements. Employers should always check state law before a layoff or reduction in force because many states have "mini-WARN Act" laws that are more burdensome than federal law.

A plant closing in the U.S. may also require a WARN notice. A plant closing is defined as a permanent or temporary shutdown of an entire facility, or the shutdown of one or more departments within a facility. The departments must have at least 50 employees (not including part-time employees) who suffer a job loss within a thirty-day period.

A mass layoff may also require a WARN notice. A mass layoff is defined as a termination (other than for cause, voluntary resignation or retirement), exceeding six months or a reduction of more than 50% of the hours employees work during each month of any six-month period. A mass layoff would result in an employment loss at the employment site during any thirty-day period of 500 or more employees or 50–499 employees if they make up at least one-third of the employer's active workforce.

As a general rule, a sale of a business is not considered a plant closing or a mass layoff unless the buyer or seller causes a plant closing or mass layoff before, during or after the sale. A seller is responsible for notice if the "layoff" occurs prior to and including the date of sale. The buyer is held responsible for all "layoffs" after the date of sale. If employees are terminated prior to a sale by the seller but are immediately hired by the buyer after the sale, the employees will not be considered to have suffered an employment loss.

Employees hired temporarily for completion of a particular project and/or part-time and seasonal or casual employees are not included in the number of employees required to be counted to determine whether WARN notice is required. A WARN notice may not be required for plant closings or other unforeseeable business circumstances which result in a layoff or termination if the layoff or termination would not have been reasonably foreseeable.

A sixty-day advanced written WARN notice must be provided to: (i) employees not represented by a union; (ii) a union representative, if applicable; (iii) a state dislocated worker unit; and (iv) the chief elected official of the local government where the employer is located and the job loss will occur.

6.3. Fines and Penalties

Failure to provide the required WARN notice could result in an employer being liable to an employee in an amount equal to back pay and benefits for the period of violation. If an employer fails to give the required notice to the unit of local government, the employer can be liable for a maximum penalty of USD 500.00 per day, up to a maximum of sixty days.

6.4. Checklist

- Employers should always review the total anticipated employment loss in the time period from ninety days before to ninety days after any job loss to determine whether a WARN notice is required.
- In reviewing any planned reductions in force or job eliminations to determine if a WARN notice is required, an employer should also consider whether any specific state and local laws and regulations may apply in a particular jurisdiction.
- Employers may also have bargaining obligations to union representatives of any employees covered by collective bargaining agreements.

7. LABOR AND EMPLOYMENT LAW RAMIFICATIONS UPON ACQUISITION OR SALE OF A BUSINESS

7.1. Overview

Employers in the U.S. are generally free to sell all or part of their business without consulting in advance with employees or their labor unions. The exceptions to this general rule are: (i) the obligation imposed by federal labor law to negotiate the *effects* of the decision with a union who represents employees of the selling business; and (ii) any obligations imposed by the WARN Act or similar state laws requiring advance notice to employees in the event of mass layoff, plant closing or sale.

In the U.S., there is a distinction between the purchase of the assets of a business and the purchase of the stock of a company. Purchasers of assets have few employment obligations in the transactional context, except laws of general applicability such as antidiscrimination laws and, in some circumstances, the obligation to consider hiring the predecessor's unionized workforce. Purchasers of a company's stock, however, are limited in the employment changes they can impose because there is generally no change in the employment relationship as a result of a stock sale.

7.2. Acquisition of a Business

7.2.1. Asset Transactions

A purchaser of the assets of a business usually is not obligated to hire any of the employees of the seller of assets unless the purchaser assumes that obligation in the Asset Purchase Agreement (APA). Nonetheless, when hiring a new workforce, a purchaser of assets often looks to the current workforce and cannot refuse to hire employees of the seller on the basis of their union membership, race, sex, religion, national origin, color, veteran's status, disability or other legally protected classification.

A purchaser of assets of a business in the U.S. should be aware of the following: (i) employees of the selling company are *not* automatically transferred to the new company that is purchasing assets; (ii) the purchasing company generally has the right to hire only those individuals it feels are best suited for the job; (iii) a purchaser of assets is normally not required to assume a collective bargaining agreement that covers employees of the selling company; (iv) a purchaser of assets may set new wages and benefits and other terms and conditions of employment for any employees it hires of the selling company; (v) if the employees of a company selling assets are represented by a labor union, the purchaser of assets is legally obligated to recognize the union only if a majority of its new workforce is comprised of former employees of the seller; and (vi) a purchaser of assets is normally not required to assume the liabilities of the selling company unless required by the APA.

As a general rule, a purchaser of assets is not required to provide advance notice to any persons prior to the closing date. However, if the purchaser of assets anticipates it will not hire the seller's employees, or if the purchaser will make substantial adverse changes to the terms and condition of employment, in some circumstances the purchaser may be required to provide advance written notice under the WARN Act or its state law equivalent.

If the employees of the selling company are represented by a union, the seller is generally not required to bargain with the union representing its employees over the decision to sell the business unless obligated to do so by the specific terms of a collective bargaining agreement. The NLRA, however, does require a seller to provide a union with sufficient advance notice to afford the union the opportunity to bargain over the *effects* of the sale (e.g., severance pay, benefits continuation and possible transfer rights). The selling company is not required to agree to all or any of a union's bargaining proposals, but it must negotiate in "good faith" with the union. Specific terms in a collective bargaining agreement may also contain restrictions on the seller (e.g., "successors and assigns" provisions requiring the seller to require the purchaser to assume the labor contract).

In a typical asset sale, the seller's employees are terminated on or before the closing date of the transaction, and the seller is normally responsible for paying any accrued but unused vacation and other benefits, as well as satisfying any "change of control" benefits in any individual employment contracts. The seller may also be obligated to provide Consolidated Omnibus Budget Reconciliation Act (COBRA) and WARN Act notices.

7.2.2. Stock Transactions

In a stock sale, the legal entity essentially remains the same. It is the identity of the shareholder(s) of the corporation who change. Unless negotiated differently in a Stock Purchase Agreement, all employment liabilities and obligations, including any existing union collective bargaining agreements, employment contracts or employee handbooks, generally become the obligation of the purchaser.

In unionized companies, after a binding letter of intent or agreement to sell is executed, the seller should notify the union representing its employees and, upon request, bargain over the "effects" of the sale. The seller should also review all employment contracts with individual nonunion employees to determine if they have any sale-related provisions.

In a typical stock transaction, there are no employment losses and WARN notices are not required by the purchaser or the seller before the closing date. However, after the stock transfer has occurred, the purchaser can terminate or lay off employees, but it cannot discriminate against any employees on the basis of any legally protected status, such as age, sex, race, religion or disability. If the new company lays off or terminates a sufficiently large number of employees, it may trigger WARN notices. If an employee decides to quit his or her job, the purchaser ordinarily does not have any obligation for severance pay or other benefits.

7.3. Pre-closing Checklist

A purchaser of stock or assets in the U.S. should always request from the seller the right to review prior to the date of closing the following types of documents (subject to a confidentiality agreement): (i) names, job titles, hire dates, employment status, salary, wage and benefits and payroll records for any current or laid-off employees; (ii) any employment applications, handbooks or other employment policies and procedures; (iii) any employment contracts or independent contractor or consultant agreements; (iv) job descriptions, evaluation, hiring and promotion guidelines; (v) union collective bargaining agreements; (vi) complaints, charges, grievances, pending or threatened lawsuits or governmental investigations; and (vii) of all profit sharing, pension, retirement, medical and any other benefit plans.

7.4. Sale of a Business

In a typical stock transaction, a buyer generally retains all employees of the seller and assumes all of the seller's employment liabilities and obligations. A seller should always first review any contracts it may have with individual employees to determine if the agreements have any sale-related provisions (e.g., "change-in-control" provisions).

As discussed above, in a typical asset sale, the seller's employees are terminated on or before the date of the sale. Consequently, the seller is normally responsible for paying any accrued and unused vacation and other accrued or vested benefits, as well as satisfying any "change of control" benefits which may be contained in individual employment contracts. The seller must also provide notice to separated employees under COBRA and in some circumstances at least sixty days' advance notice of employment separations under the WARN Act or similar state laws. Employees of the seller who are not terminated as of the closing date normally become the purchaser's employees and do not suffer an "employment loss."

A seller with union employees is generally not required to bargain with a union representing its employees over the decision to sell a business. Sellers are required, however, to provide union(s) with advance notice of a sale to afford the union(s) a meaningful opportunity to bargain over the effects of the transaction (e.g., severance pay, insurance continuation, transfer rights). A seller is not obligated to agree to any of a union's "effects" bargaining proposals but must negotiate in "good faith." Some collective bargaining agreements may also contain specific requirements or restrictions on the seller (e.g., "successors and assigns" clause requiring the seller to obtain the buyer's assumption of the labor contract).

7.5. Checklist

Any employer in the U.S. that sells a business should remember that: (i) employees may be entitled to certain pay or other benefits in the event of a sale or closing of a business in accordance with written policies and procedures or a union labor contract; (ii) employees may be entitled to continue their group health insurance in accordance with COBRA; and (iii) federal or state laws or a union collective bargaining agreement may require the seller of a business to give employees advance written notice.

8. USE OF ALTERNATIVE WORKFORCES IN THE U.S.: INDEPENDENT CONTRACTORS, JOINT EMPLOYERS, CONTRACT EMPLOYEES AND TEMPORARY OR LEASED WORKERS

8.1. Overview

The costs of using workers who are not employees are typically less than the cost of employees. For example, if a company uses nonemployee workers, it may be able to reduce costs by: (i) not making contributions for Medicare, Social Security or unemployment insurance; (ii) not providing workers' compensation benefits; and (iii) not paying overtime. In addition, the relationship with workers who are not employees is often more flexible.

8.2. Independent Contractors

Individuals who are properly classified as independent contractors are not employees and not subject to Fair Labor Standards Act (FLSA) requirements relating to minimum wage, overtime, and recordkeeping. They perform their work based on a contract which specifies their compensation and other terms and conditions. Simply calling a person an independent contractor does not automatically make the person an independent contractor. To determine whether a person is truly an independent contractor requires an analysis of, among other things, how much control the company has over the contractor and the manner in which contractor's work is done; whether the contractor or the company provides supplies and tools; how the contractor is paid; and whether and what type of policies may apply to the relationship. While the legal tests may vary from state to state, key issues to evaluate are whether the company is exercising significant control over the contractor's day-to-day performance of the job; whether the contractor has any risk of financial loss, and whether the contractor works for other companies.

There should always be a written agreement between the company and the independent contractor to evidence the type of relationship. This agreement should specify the work requirements for the particular job; a start and end date; and the conditions for contract termination. Importantly, the contract should state that the person is an independent contractor—not an employee—and the contractor will not be eligible for benefits that are afforded to employees or the company.

Independent contractors are not paid an hourly wage or salary similar to employees. Rather, they are only paid the compensation in their agreement. Although an independent contractor may have obligations to pay wages, benefits and salary to its own employees, the company using the contractor's services is not liable for wages and benefits to the contractor's employees.

Notably, the U.S. Department of Labor (DOL) has proposed a new rule for the test to determine whether a worker is an employee under the FLSA or independent contractor that we anticipated will be implemented as proposed. Rather than the current multifactor test that emphasizes two core factors—the nature and degree of the worker's control over the work and the worker's opportunity for profit or loss—, the new rule would impose a six-factor "totality-of-the-circumstances" test to broaden the definition of employee. These factors include: (i) the worker's opportunity for profit or loss depending on managerial skill; (ii) investment by the worker and the employer (i.e., whether a worker's investment is "capital or entrepreneurial in nature"); (iii) degree of permanence of the work relationship; (iv) nature and degree of the employer's control, including reserved control, over the performance of the work and the economic aspects of the working relationship; (v) whether work performed is an "integral" part of the employer's business; and (vi) skill and initiative (i.e., whether the worker uses specialized skills to perform the work and whether those skills contribute to business-like initiative). Under the new rule, an employee is broadly defined as any individual whom an employer "suffers, permits, or otherwise employs to work" and would encompass all workers who "as a matter of economic reality, are economically dependent on an employer for work." Additionally, an independent contractor is only a worker who is, as a matter of economic reality, "in business for themselves."

8.3. Joint Employer Rule

Over the years, the joint employer rule has always required that for an independent business entity to be deemed joint employer of another company's employees, such independent business entity must actually exercise control over such other company's employees. Recently, however, the NLRB finalized a new rule that provides an independent business entity may be deemed joint employer of another company's employees if it exercises the power to control (whether directly, indirectly, or both) or even merely because it has authority to control (whether directly, indirectly, or both) any essential term or condition of their employment, regardless of whether it ever actually exercises such control.

The new rule further significantly expands the current rule's definition of the "essential terms and conditions of employment" by including additional terms that are inherently vague, meaning that it will now be far more likely for one business to be deemed a joint employer of another business's employees under the NLRA. Now, the definition of the "essential terms and conditions of employment" includes: "(1) wages, benefits, and other compensation; (2) hours of work and scheduling; (3) the assignment of duties to be performed; (4) the supervision of the performance of duties; (5) work rules and directions governing the manner, means, and methods of the performance of duties and the grounds for discipline; (6) the tenure of employment, including hiring and discharge; and (7) working conditions related to the safety and health of employees."[1] In addition, the new rule requires that a joint employer of a group of employees "must bargain collectively with the representative of those employees with respect to any term and condition of employment that it possesses the authority to control or exercises the power to control, regardless of whether that term or condition is deemed to be an essential term and condition of employment..."[2] This means that under the new rule, joint employers must bargain regarding the employment relationship and can be held liable for unfair labor practices involving workers they did not believe were their employees.

Now, all employers should review their current and pending contracts with other independent businesses to determine whether those agreements could be considered reserving the authority to potentially control any essential term or condition of another entity's employees. They should also consider performing an internal audit to review the practices and procedures of their supervisors and managers and train them to avoid actions that may arguably be considered direct or indirect control over another entity's employees.

8.4. Temporary and Leased Workers

Temporary and leased workers are individuals who are usually hired for a short or fixed period of time. Companies may hire such workers directly or lease them through a third-party agency.

A temporary worker is an individual who is hired directly by the company for a short period of time. This person is usually an employee—not an independent contractor. Temporary workers may be excluded from participating in certain benefit plans that the company provides to its regular full-time employees.

Leased workers are generally employed by a third-party company (such as a staffing agency). Leased workers are employees of the third-party company. Companies should be aware, however, that exercising control over leased workers may give rise to a joint employer relationship, and the leased worker could be deemed an employee of both the company and the temporary agency.

1. 29 CFR 103.40(d).
2. 29 CFR 103.40(h)(1).

To avoid a joint employer relationship for a leased worker, a company should minimize its role in selecting or terminating the services of the leased worker. For example, a company could provide a job description to the third-party staffing company, but the staffing company would be responsible for supplying workers as needed. Additionally, a written agreement should be negotiated with the staffing company that provides: (i) the leasing or staffing company is responsible for the recruitment, interviewing, hiring and firing; (ii) the staffing agency is responsible for paying wages, overtime and making the appropriate tax deductions and maintaining payroll records and providing workers' compensation coverage; and (iii) the leasing company will indemnify and hold harmless the contracting company for any claims made by the employees of the leasing company.

Employers should also review emerging state laws that purport to restrict the long-term use of staffing company employees and that effectively treat long-term staffing company workers as de facto employees. For example, Illinois' new amendments to its Day and Temporary Labor Services Act[3] enhanced temporary workers' equal pay rights and protections by (i) mandating that day and temporary labor service agencies (a.k.a. "temp agencies") provide temporary workers assigned to a third-party client for more than ninety calendar days with benefits and pay at least as in the same amount as the comparable lowest paid employee directly hired by the third-party client; (ii) requiring both temp agencies and third-party clients provide temporary workers with training specific to the job site at which they have been assigned to work; (iii) giving temporary workers the right to refuse an assignment to a worksite where a strike, lockout or other "labor trouble" exists; and (iv) expanding the Act's private right of action by granting additional parties the ability to initiate a civil action for a violation of the Act.

9. OBLIGATION TO BARGAIN COLLECTIVELY WITH TRADE UNIONS: EMPLOYEES' RIGHT TO STRIKE AND A COMPANY'S RIGHT TO CONTINUE BUSINESS OPERATIONS

9.1. Overview

In the U.S., unions represent only approximately 14 million employees and the number of union employees working for private sector employers has dropped to less than 10% of the total workforce in the U.S.

3. 820 ILCS 175.

9.2. Right of Employees to Join Unions

The NLRA establishes procedures for employees of private companies (other than employees of railroads and airlines who are covered by the Railway Labor Act) to select and bargain with a union representative of their own choosing for purposes of establishing terms and conditions of employment. The NLRA is administered and enforced by the NLRB.

The NLRA applies, but is not limited to, the following types of private companies in the U.S.: industrial businesses; factories and warehouses; retail establishments; private colleges and universities; transportation and logistics businesses; hospitals and health care institutions; hotels and motels; apartment and office buildings; shopping centers; radio, television and newspapers; restaurants; and technology companies.

9.3. How Employees Select a Union

In the U.S., unions must obtain the consent of employees to represent them. After a union has obtained the support of a majority of employees in an appropriate bargaining unit, a union may demand that the employer recognizes it as the bargaining representative of that group of employees. An employer in the U.S. may recognize the union on the basis of signed authorization cards, but the employer may also insist that the NLRB conducts a secret-ballot election to determine if employees really want a union to be their representative.

To start the NLRB secret-ballot election process, a union or employees must file an election petition with the NLRB, supported by the signatures of at least 30% of employees within an appropriate bargaining unit. As a general rule, an appropriate bargaining unit consists of all of the employees at a single site of employment who have a substantial community of interest. If the cards or petition are signed by 30% or more of the employees in the unit, the NLRB will quickly order a secret-ballot election, usually within twenty-five to forty-five days of filing the petition. A similar procedure exists for employees who wish to cancel the union as their bargaining representative, referred to as "decertification."

If a majority of the eligible employees who cast a ballot in an NLRB election, vote for union representation, the union is "certified" as the bargaining representative of those employees. The employer must then engage in "good faith" collective bargaining with the union over terms and conditions of employment (wages, hours and working conditions).

9.4. Preelection Campaigning

Both unions and companies have the right to meet with employees prior to an NLRB election and discuss whether they want to join a union or not. After a petition is filed with the NLRB, companies and unions can meet with employees to conduct a "campaign" and address the advantages and disadvantages of unionization. As a general rule, unions cannot meet with employees on the premises of the employer.

During an election campaign, companies are prohibited from: (i) making any threats to employees, such as discharge, layoff, loss of pay, loss of benefits, if the employee votes for the union; (ii) asking employees whether they signed a card, how they intend to vote or whether they support the union; (iii) promising an employee better wages, benefits or working conditions if the employee votes against the union; (iv) "spying" on union activity; or (v) visiting employees in their homes.

9.5. Company Unfair Labor Practices

Employees who work for most private sector companies in the U.S. have the right to form or join a labor organization for purposes of collective bargaining free from any threats or coercion. Accordingly, companies are prohibited (even if there is no union petition or organizing activity) from: (i) questioning employees about their union activities; (ii) promising or implementing wage increases to discourage union activity or support; (iii) threatening to close a plant or lay off employees to discourage union activity; (iv) threatening employees with loss of benefits; (v) discharging, disciplining or taking any action against an employee because of his or her support for a union; and/or (vi) restricting employees from talking or communicating with each other about gripes at work or terms and conditions of employment.

The NLRB imposes restriction even on nonunion companies in the U.S. such as: (i) they may not discriminate between the posting of union and other nonwork-related materials; (ii) they may not prohibit the distribution of union materials in work areas and solicitation of employees to sign union cards during working time, unless the employer prohibits all forms of nonwork-related distribution and solicitation during work time; (iii) they may not refuse to hire an applicant because the applicant is or has been a union member; and (iv) they may not prohibit employees from discussing their wages, hours of work or working conditions.

9.6. Union Unfair Labor Practices

The NLRB, for example, also prohibits unions from engaging in certain conduct. Thus, unions may not picket secondary employers, picket a primary employer for more than thirty days for recognition unless it files for an election, fail to bargain in good faith or threaten employees. An unfair labor practice charge can be filed by an employer or the employee. The NLRB may seek an injunction in federal district court against unlawful picketing.

9.7. Relocation of Work/Shutdown of Business

If employees are represented by a union, an employer is generally obligated to engage in good faith bargaining with a union *before* making a final decision about: (i) contracting out, moving, relocating or outsourcing work for labor costs which may result in a job loss; and/or (ii) laying-off employees or eliminating jobs for labor costs.

In contrast, an employer is generally not obligated to bargain with a union before making a final decision as to the sale or closing of a business unless such obligations are contained in a collective bargaining agreement. As a general rule, however, unless the collective bargaining agreement contains a specific waiver, an employer should bargain with a union over both the "decision" and also the "effects" of any business decisions which may result in job losses for any reasons relating to labor costs.

9.8. Checklist

- Employees of private companies have the right to act in concert even in the absence of a union.
- Employees of private companies may designate a union as their collective bargaining representative by voting in a secret-ballot election conducted by the NLRB.
- An employer must bargain with a union lawfully elected by a majority of its employees and negotiate in good faith over wages, benefits and other terms and conditions of employment. In some states, union agreements may require employees to become members of the union and/or pay monthly dues or an administrative fee to the union as a condition of employment.
- Prior to and during a union election campaign, a company has the right to discuss the disadvantages of unions and expresses its opinion why it is opposed to a union representing the employees in its workforce.

- A union can meet with employees outside of work hours and pass out information off the employer's premises explaining why it believes that employees should vote for unionization.
- As a general rule, a company should notify the union representing its employees of any future plans which may impact jobs and be prepared to negotiate with the union about both the "decision" and the "effect" of the decision on employees, unless clearly waived by the union in the written bargaining agreement.

10. WORKING CONDITIONS: HOURS OF WORK AND PAYMENT OF WAGES: BY STATUTE OR COLLECTIVE AGREEMENTS

10.1. Overview of Wage and Hour Laws

Hours of work and payment of wages in the U.S. are controlled by overlapping regulations at the federal, state and local levels of government. At the federal level, the FLSA sets minimum standards for employees in all states.

Most states and some municipalities also have their own laws that also regulate minimum wage and hours requirements. These laws may provide additional benefits to employees greater than the requirements of the FLSA. Additional regulations may be imposed for employees who work on government-funded projects.

Some wage/hour requirements may be modified pursuant to an individual employment contract or a collective bargaining agreement. However, most federal and state wage/hour requirements are considered nonwaivable and cannot be modified by agreement.

10.2. Minimum Wages

The FLSA establishes minimum wage requirements for employees in the U.S. The current federal minimum wage is USD 7.25 per hour, but this is likely to increase. For employers of "tipped" employees, employees can elect to use the "tip credit" where the current federal minimum wage is USD 2.13 per hour. Employers can only use the tip credit subject to the 80/20 rule, where the tip-producing employee spends at least 80% of workweek hours on tip-producing work and no more than 20%—or thirty continuous minutes—of workweek hours on tasks that directly support tip-producing activities. The DOL's Wage and Hour Division administers and enforces the federal minimum wage laws.

Many states and municipalities set higher minimum wage rates. For example, in California, the minimum wage is USD 15.50 per hour. If a state or municipality has a minimum wage law higher than the federal law or state law, the employee is entitled to receive the highest applicable minimum rate. There are also federal and state laws which require employees working on certain public works projects to be paid the "prevailing wage rate" as determined by the applicable government entity.

10.3. Overtime

In accordance with federal law, hourly nonexempt employees are entitled to receive overtime pay for all hours worked over forty in a workweek. A "workweek" is defined as a fixed and regularly recurring period—seven consecutive twenty-four-hour periods. An employer may designate when a workweek begins and ends. The workweek need not coincide with the calendar week. If the employer does not designate its workweek, the default workweek starts at 12:01 a.m. on Sunday and ends at midnight the following Saturday.

The federal rate for overtime work in excess of forty hours in a workweek is equal to one and one-half times an employee's regular rate of pay. The employee's "regular rate" of pay for overtime is not limited to his or her base salary or hourly rate but may also include other types of compensation for work performed. For example, an employee's "regular rate" of pay may include commissions, production or incentive bonuses, prizes (if awarded for work quality, quantity or efficiency) and other forms of compensation.

The FLSA does not automatically require overtime pay for work performed on Saturdays, Sundays, holidays or regular days of rest if the total hours worked in the workweek do not exceed forty hours.

Several states, however, have overtime laws that are more restrictive than the FLSA. For example, in California, overtime at one and one-half rate must be paid for work in excess of either eight hours per day or forty hours per week. Overtime at the double rate must be paid for work in excess of twelve hours per day. Additionally, when an employee in California is required to work all seven days of the same workweek, the employee is entitled to overtime on the seventh day at the one and one-half rate for the first eight hours, and overtime at the double rate after eight hours. A "workday" is defined as eight hours in a consecutive twenty-four-hour period beginning at the same time each calendar day, but it may begin at any time of day.

10.4. Meal and Rest Periods

The FLSA does not require employers to provide meal periods or rest breaks to employees. However, when employers do offer short breaks (usually lasting from five to twenty minutes), the breaks are considered work hours that are included in the number of hours worked during the workweek for the purposes of calculating hours worked and overtime.

When employers provide uninterrupted bona fide meal periods typically lasting at least thirty minutes, these meal periods are not work time and are not compensable. The employer must be able to verify, however, that employees were actually relieved of all job duties for the entire meal period. If employees are required to perform any work during meal or rest periods, whether active or inactive (e.g., remaining at their workstations while eating), the employer runs a risk that the meal period will be deemed compensable and count as hours worked.

Some states have more stringent laws that expressly require employers to provide meal periods or rest breaks to employees. Some states, such as California, require employers to provide both meal periods and rest breaks on a daily basis.

10.5. Deductions from Wages

Employers are required to withhold various taxes from employee paychecks, including federal income taxes, state income taxes (if applicable), and Social Security taxes. These deductions are statutorily mandated by the Internal Revenue Code and other federal and state statutes.

Other deductions from paychecks may be permitted in limited circumstances. For example, an employee may be subject to a wage garnishment order (discussed below), or the employee may voluntarily authorize certain deductions to enroll in employee benefits, make retirement contributions or other purposes. Even when permitted, however, certain deductions cannot reduce the employee's pay below the minimum wage or overtime pay requirements.

10.6. Garnishment

When an employee's wages become subject to a garnishment order, the federal Consumer Credit Protection Act prohibits employers from terminating employment because of a garnishment and restricts the amount of money that can be garnished. The maximum amount of wages that may be garnished in any workweek or payroll period generally is the lesser of: (i)

25% of disposable earnings (earnings after statutory withholdings); and/or (ii) the amount by which disposable earnings are greater than thirty times the federal minimum hourly wage in effect at the time the earnings are payable. Some states also have laws imposing greater restrictions on wage garnishments.

10.7. Exemptions to Wage and Hour Laws

Certain categories of employees are exempt from coverage of the FLSA, as well as state wage/hour laws. Some exemptions apply solely to overtime pay requirements, and other exemptions apply to both the minimum wage and overtime pay requirements. Qualifications for various exemptions typically consider the duties the employee primarily performs, the employee's compensation and the employer's industry. Exemptions are narrowly construed against the employer. This means that employers should carefully review the criteria of any exemption to determine if it applies to any employees. Some states impose additional requirements for exemptions to state wage and hour laws.

The most common exemptions to overtime and minimum wage requirements are the "white collar" exemptions. These are applicable to employees holding executive, administrative or professional positions. Most of these exemptions have both a duties test and a wage threshold test—neither the job title itself nor the fact that the employee is on salary is determinative. The employer has the burden of establishing the exemption.

Entitlement to "white collar" exemptions usually requires that employees all be paid on a salary basis. To be paid on a "salary basis" means that the employee receives a predetermined weekly salary that is not subject to reduction based upon the quality or quantity of work. The predetermined salary may be reduced in less than full-week increments only in very narrow circumstances.

Currently, the "white collar" exemptions to the FLSA (and some similar state laws) are as follows:

(i) *Executive Exemption:* (1) the employee's primary duty consists of management of the business or a recognized department or subdivision; (2) the employee customarily and regularly directs the work of two or more full-time employees or their equivalent; (3) the employee has the authority to hire or fire other employees or his or her recommendations as to hiring, firing, promotion or other change of status of other employees are given particular weight; and (4) the employee is paid on a salary or fee basis at a rate of at least USD 684.00 per week.

(ii) *Administrative Exemption:* (1) the employee's primary duty consists of the performance of office or nonmanual work directly related to the management or general business operations of the company or the employer's customers; (2) the employee customarily and regularly exercises discretion and independent judgment with respect to matters of significance; and (3) the employee is paid on a salary or fee basis at a rate of at least USD 684.00 per week.

(iii) *Professional Exemptions:*

Learned Professional: (1) the employee's primary duty consists of work requiring advanced knowledge (work, i.e., predominantly intellectual in character and includes work requiring consistent exercise of discretion and judgment); and (2) the advanced knowledge is in a field of science or learning; (3) the advanced knowledge is customarily acquired by a prolonged course of specialized intellectual instruction (as opposed to a general academic education, an apprenticeship, or training in the performance of routine mental, manual or physical processes); and (4) the employee is paid on a salary or fee basis at a rate of at least USD 684.00 per week, unless the employee is a bona fide practitioner in law or medicine.

Creative Professional: (1) the employee's primary duty consists of work that requires invention, imagination or talent of the employee in a recognized field of artistic endeavor (as opposed to work that can be produced by a person with general manual or intellectual ability and training); and (2) the employee is paid on a salary or fee basis at a rate of at least USD 684.00 per week.

Computer Professional: (1) the employee is employed as a computer systems analyst, computer programmer, software engineer or other similarly skilled workers; (2) the employee's primary duty consists of: (a) the application of systems analysis techniques and procedures, including consulting with users to determine hardware, software or system functional specifications; (b) the design, development, documentation, analysis, creation, testing or modification of computer systems or programs, including prototypes, based on and related to user or system design specifications; (c) the design, documentation, testing, creation or modification of computer programs relating to machine operating systems; or (d) a combination of the above duties, the performance of which requires the same level of skills; and (3) the employee is paid either on a salary or fee basis at a rate of at least USD 684.00 per week or on an hourly basis at a rate of at least USD 27.63 per hour.

(iv) *Highly Compensated Employee Exemption:* (1) the employee's primary duty includes performing office or nonmanual work; (2) the employee customarily and regularly performs at least one of the exempt duties or responsibilities of an exempt executive, administrative or professional employee; and (3) the employee is paid total annual compensation of USD 107,432.00 or more, which includes at least USD 684.00 per week paid on a salary or fee basis.

(v) *Outside Sales Employee Exemption:* (1) the employee's primary duty consists of making sales, or obtaining orders or contracts for services or for the use of facilities for which a consideration will be paid by the customer; and (2) the employee is customarily and regularly engaged away from the employer's place of business. There are no specific compensation requirements to qualify for this exemption.

(vi) *Commissioned Employee Exemption:* (1) the employee works for a retail or service establishment; (2) the employee's regular rate of pay is in excess of one and one-half times the minimum wage; and (3) more than half of the employee's compensation consists of commissions on goods or services.

However, on April 23, 2024, the Department of Labor issued a final rule updating the wage thresholds for executive, administrative and professionals as well as highly compensated employees starting on July 1, 2024 and updating again on January 1, 2025. For the executive, administrative and professional exemptions, the wage threshold will increase on July 1, 2024 to at least USD 844.00 per week on a salary or fee basis and thereafter on January 1, 2025 to at least USD 1,128.00 per week on a salary or fee basis. For highly compensated employees, the wage threshold will increase on July 1, 2024 to a total annual compensation of USD 132,964.00 or more, which includes at least USD 844.00 per week paid on a salary or fee basis and thereafter on January 1, 2025 to a total annual compensation of USD 151,164.00 or more, which includes at least USD 1,128.00 per week paid on a salary or fee basis. On top of these updates, beginning July 1, 2027, the wage thresholds will update every three years and are set to be calculated by applying up-to-date wage data to determine the new wage levels.

Some states have adopted similar exemptions or do not allow some or all of the federal exemptions, or modify the requirements needed to qualify for them. If an employee is subject to both federal and state laws, state law must be followed when it is more favorable to the employee in order to ensure compliance with both the federal and state wage law requirements.

10.8. Child Labor

The DOL enforces federal child labor laws, pursuant to the FLSA. Restrictions generally are based on the age of the minor (an individual under age 18) and the type of work involved. An individual who reaches age of 18 is no longer subject to child labor laws.

As a general rule, age 14 is the minimum age for employment in the U.S. Some specific jobs are exempt from child labor laws and may be performed by minors under age 14. The FLSA provides that 14- and 15-year-old workers may work outside school hours in specified nonmanufacturing, non-mining, nonhazardous jobs under certain conditions. Permissible work hours for 14- and 15-year-old workers are three hours on a school day, eighteen hours in a school week, eight hours on a non-school day, and forty hours in a non-school week. Their work must be performed between 7:00 a.m. and 7:00 p.m., except from June 1, through Labor Day (the first Monday in September) for which evening work hours are extended to 9:00 p.m.

Under the FLSA, 16- and 17-year-old workers may be employed for an unlimited number of hours in any occupation other than those specifically designated by the DOL as too hazardous for minors. Several states impose restrictions on the number of hours and times of day that minors aged 16 and 17 may work.

Each state also has its own laws relating to the employment of minors. If state law and FLSA overlap, the law which is more protective of the minor will apply.

10.9. Record-Keeping Requirements

Employers are required to keep comprehensive payroll records for at least three years (or longer, depending on state law).

The DOL's three-year record-keeping requirement does not relieve the employer of its separate obligation under the Internal Revenue Code to maintain certain tax-related employee pay records for four years after the tax due date or date taxes are paid.

Some states impose additional record-keeping requirements. In California, for example, employers are required to, among other things, maintain records showing: (i) the times that nonexempt employees start and end each meal and work period (including split shift intervals); (ii) total daily hours worked; (iii) total hours worked in the pay period; and (iv) additional compensation information.

Employers may also keep employment records for longer periods than the required minimum, based on the applicable statutes of limitations for employment-related claims in the jurisdictions where their employees work.

Other considerations may make it advisable for an employer to retain pay-related records for a longer period. For example, some employers may keep pay records for substantially longer periods in view of the Lilly Ledbetter Fair Pay Act of 2009, which changed the statute of limitations applicable to a pay discrimination claim. While the Act restricts back-pay awards to two years, the Act provides that the federal statute of limitations for challenging a discriminatory pay practice (either 180 days or 300 days) starts again each time the employee receives a paycheck reflecting the alleged discriminatory practice. This means that new discrimination claims can be based on pay decisions made many years earlier.

Some states also require employers to furnish itemized wage statements to employees each time they make a wage payment. In California, for example, the itemized wage statements must show: (i) gross wages earned; (ii) total hours worked (except for exempt employees who are paid solely on a salary basis); (iii) the number of piece-rate units earned and any applicable piece-rate if the employee is paid on a piece-rate basis; (iv) all deductions; (v) net and gross wages earned; (vi) inclusive dates for the payroll period in which the employee is being paid; (vii) the employee's name and either the last four digits of his or her social security number or an employee identification number; (viii) the name and address of the legal entity that is the employer; and (ix) all applicable hourly rates in effect during the payroll period and the corresponding number of hours worked at each hourly rate by the employee.

An employer who fails to maintain accurate work records runs a risk of being responsible for what the employee contends such records would have shown. Employee testimony as to his or her actual hours of work generally will prevail if the employer fails to maintain the required records.

10.10. Changes to an Employee's Wages and Benefits

Wages and benefits for at-will employees may be changed or reduced at any time in the future by providing notice of the reduction before the employees perform work at the new rate. Reductions in pay may in some cases not be allowed if employees are covered by employment contracts or union collective bargaining agreements (i.e., employees who are not employed at-will). In addition, pay reductions can never reduce an employee's compensation below the applicable federal or state minimum wage.

Reducing an exempt employee's pay may also violate the "salary basis" test required for the most common exemptions and render the employee eligible for overtime pay. FLSA regulations provide that a salaried exempt employee must receive his or her full salary for performing any work in the workweek, except in very limited circumstances. An exempt employee's pay also cannot be reduced below the minimum threshold required to qualify for the exemption.

10.11. Checklist

- In addition to federal wage and hour laws, employers *must* also comply with overlapping state and local laws that regulate the hours of work and pay for employees within those jurisdictions.
- Employees must be paid at least the applicable minimum wage or, if exempt, at least the amount (and manner of compensation) required to qualify for an applicable exemption under the FLSA and state law.
- Nonexempt hourly employees must be paid overtime for work in excess of forty hours per week at a rate of one and one-half times the regular rate of pay (or in accordance with more stringent state laws where applicable).
- Employees must be relieved of all duties when taking unpaid meal or rest periods.
- Statutorily mandated deductions must be withheld from an employee's wages.
- Employees who are classified as exempt under the FLSA and state laws must meet all elements of the test for the applicable exemption.
- Accurate records of employee compensation and hours worked must be maintained a minimum of three years for most payroll records, and a minimum four years after the tax due date or date taxes are paid for certain tax-related pay records, or possibly longer periods for certain records depending on the jurisdictions where the employees work.

11. OTHER WORKING CONDITIONS AND BENEFITS: BY STATUTE, COLLECTIVE AGREEMENTS OR COMPANY POLICY

Benefits offered by employers to their employees in the U.S. are traditionally a significant part of the employees' compensation and benefits are used to attract and retain employees in the U.S. However, with the exception of paying governmental mandated benefits (e.g., Social Security and Medicare), discussed below, private employers generally are not required to provide health and welfare or retirement benefits to their employees. The

2010 Patient Protection and Affordable Care Act, as modified by the Health Care and Education Reconciliation Act of 2010 (together the "Health Care Act"), may, however, require certain employers to pay penalties if they do not provide an "affordable" health plan that provides an "essential" level of benefits to their employees and covered family members.

U.S. Laws Covering Health and Welfare and Retirement Benefits

Many employee benefit plans an employer wants to provide to its employees must comply with the Internal Revenue Code of 1986, as amended (the Code), in order to qualify for favorable tax treatment. In addition, the majority of health and welfare plans and retirement plans must also comply with the applicable provisions of the Employee Retirement Income Security Act of 1974, as amended (ERISA).

The Code

The Code establishes the federal taxation, withholding and reporting requirements with respect to various types of employee benefit programs. Some programs may be provided on a tax-free basis, and others, if structured correctly, can provide for the deferral of tax on the benefit. Both health benefits and qualified retirement benefits may be subject to nondiscrimination testing under the Code. Penalties and less-favorable tax treatment may apply to those programs that fail nondiscrimination testing as a result of providing more favorable benefits to those employees who meet a statutory definition of "highly compensated" than those who would be considered "non-highly compensated."

ERISA

Under ERISA, employer-sponsored plans may be required to disclose information regarding plan features and funding to employees and provide employees with a claims process for obtaining benefits. ERISA also creates fiduciary duties for the individuals who manage and control assets of certain types of plans and establishes the right of employees to sue for benefits and breaches of fiduciary duty. Fiduciaries who do not follow the fiduciary principles of conduct may be personally liable to restore any losses to the plan or to disgorge any profits made through improper use of plan assets. Courts may take whatever action is appropriate against fiduciaries who breach their duties under ERISA, including their removal. In addition, ERISA may preempt state and local laws applicable to health and welfare and retirement plans other than certain state insurance laws. Plans covered by ERISA are generally also subject to various annual reporting requirements to the government.

11.1. Health and Other Insurance

Many employers offer a wide variety of health and welfare benefits to their employees, including, but not limited to, medical and dental care (often including surgical care and hospital stays), vision plans, and benefits due to accident, illness, disability or death. Federal and state governments also provide health and welfare benefits to certain individuals who meet certain eligibility requirements. Although private employers are not required to offer benefits, depending upon the industry, the employee may expect to be offered various benefits in connection with employment. Moreover, as a result of the Health Care Act, employers of a certain size will be subject to penalties if they do not provide certain levels of health care benefits at a reasonable cost. Further, if the employer offers health benefits, ERISA mandates include a prohibition against discriminating against employees and others on the basis of their health status, claims experience, genetic information or disability when it comes to enrollment or costs, minimum hospital stays for mothers and newborns, and parity for mental health and substance abuse benefits when compared to medical and surgical benefits. Health care plans may, and frequently do, exclude from participation part-time employees. Health care plans may be self-funded by the employer or provided through insurance; however, regardless of the funding mechanism, these benefits are strictly regulated under ERISA, the Code and various other federal statutes as further described below.

Self-Funded Plans

In a self-funded plan, the employer assumes the financial risk for providing benefits to the employees covered under the plan and directly pays the claims covered under the plan. The employer may establish a separate trust to fund benefits or make payments from its general assets. Further, although "stop-loss" insurance is often purchased in order to protect the employer from extremely large unexpected claims, the employer bears the risk of plan solvency. (Under a stop-loss policy, the employer is responsible for the payment of all benefits up to a certain level, which may be established on a plan or per person basis.) Employees may or may not be required to pay a premium to defray the cost of coverage.

Self-funded plans are often cheaper than insured plans because the employer is not obligated to pay for the administrative costs and profits of the insurer. Self-funded plans allow the employer additional flexibility in determining plan design and coverage, which may make them more difficult to administer. Employers with self-funded plans typically hire a third party to assist with the administration of the plan. Self-funded plans are also not subject to state insurance regulation. Self-funded health plans are subject to nondiscrimination testing in order for the benefits to be provided on a tax-free basis to employees. The testing rules prohibit discrimination in either eligibility for, or access to, the benefits.

Insured Arrangements

Insured arrangements provide health care and other welfare benefits, such as disability and life insurance, through large insurance providers. Typically, the employer pays a premium for each employee, all or a portion of which may be charged back to the employee subject to the cost requirements of the Health Care Act as it relates to group health insurance. The insurance company manages the administration of the program, including claims processing.

Types of Benefits Offered

The following types of benefits may be offered under either a self-funded plan, insured plan or a combination thereof:

- *Medical Plan:* In the U.S., medical coverage is often provided by the employer. Depending upon the industry, the employee may expect to receive individual or family coverage as part of the employee's compensation package. A medical plan typically covers a broad range of services, which may include doctor visits, hospitalization, physical therapy, mental evaluations, pharmaceuticals, rehabilitation care and therapy and prevention and wellness programs.
- *Dental and Vision:* Many companies offer their employees dental and/or vision coverage. These may be offered through the medical plan or as separate benefits.
- *COBRA:* The Consolidated Omnibus Budget Reconciliation Act of 1985 (COBRA), as amended, gives employees and their families the right to choose to continue the group health benefits provided by their employers' group health plans for limited periods of time if coverage is otherwise lost due to certain circumstances (e.g., job loss, reduction in hours worked, transition between jobs, death, divorce and other life events). Employers with twenty or more employees who sponsor group health plans are required to offer qualified employees and their qualified dependents the opportunity to extend coverage at a cost of no more than 102% of the cost of coverage under the plan. In addition, certain states may have their own continuation coverage statutes, which, if more generous, will apply to group health benefit plans.
- *Life Insurance and Accidental Death and Dismemberment:* Employers may purchase group term life insurance for their employees. Generally, the cost of the first USD 50,000.00 of this type of insurance coverage can be paid for by the employer on a tax-free basis (e.g., the cost of the benefit is not included in the gross income of the employees) if certain

requirements are met. The cost of coverage in excess of USD 50,000.00 will generally result in imputed income to the employee.

- *Disability Insurance:* Disability insurance is an income-replacement benefit for employees who are unable to work due to medical issues. Employees may receive coverage on a short-term or long-term basis. The benefit may provide partial or full income replacement and employers have wide discretion in defining "disability" as long as the definition is applied on a uniform basis.
- *Cafeteria Plans:* Cafeteria plans offer employees the chance to make pretax contributions toward the cost of their welfare benefits. These plans usually allow the employee to make selections from a "menu" of benefits, allowing some level of customization.
- *Health Care Act:* The Health Care Act establishes a federally mandated health care system that became effective gradually over a period of several years between 2010 and 2018. The Health Care Act does not require employers to offer group health plans to their employees, but it does impose cash penalties on employers with at least 50 full-time employees who fail to offer "affordable" health plans that provide an "essential" level of benefits to their employees and covered family members. Large employers that fail to offer such coverage will be subject to a penalty if any of their full-time employees secure subsidized coverage on a state health care exchange. The amount of the penalty will depend on whether the employer fails to offer minimum essential coverage to some or all of its full-time employees or offers coverage that is not affordable.

Under the Health Care Act, various coverage requirements were phased in over several years. Among the mandated benefits are coverage of adult children (up to age 26) of covered employees, prohibition of annual and lifetime limits on benefits, elimination of coverage exclusions for preexisting conditions and automatic enrollment of employees after permitted waiting periods expire. Although it is likely many employers will offer these programs going forward, the states are required to establish insurance exchanges for individuals who do not have coverage and employees of small employers.

Governmental and Other Benefits

Governmental Benefits

Although health and welfare benefits in the U.S. are traditionally provided through the employer, the Federal and state governments also offer qualifying individuals certain health and welfare benefits through the Medicare, Medicaid, Social Security Disability Insurance (SSDI) and Unemployment Insurance (UI) programs:

- *Medicaid:* Medicaid is a health insurance program that is jointly funded by the state and Federal governments. It is available for certain individuals with disabilities as well as individuals with limited income and resources. The rules for determining eligibility, the scope of coverage, and the cost of services are determined at the state level. Medicaid beneficiaries may pay nominal deductibles, coinsurance, or copayments, depending on the state, but the program is otherwise funded by states, and the states are then reimbursed by the Federal government for a share of their Medicaid expenditures.
- *Medicare:* Medicare is health insurance provided by the Federal government generally for people 65 or older or people under 65 with disabilities. Medicare is available to people who have entered the U.S. lawfully and lived in the country for at least five years. Medicare has several components, including hospital insurance, medical insurance and prescription drug benefits. Medicare is funded through payroll taxes, which are typically split between employers and employees.
- *SSDI:* Social Security Disability Insurance pays benefits to the disabled and certain covered family members. A disabled individual becomes insured by working and paying Social Security taxes for a certain amount of time. Monthly payments begin after an individual becomes disabled and generally continue until the medical condition has improved and the individual can work again.
- *UI:* Unemployment Insurance is a social insurance program that operates at both the state and federal levels. Each state administers a UI program within guidelines established by Federal law. UI programs provide payments to individuals who are unemployed, generally through no fault of their own, and who continually meet certain eligibility requirements. Benefits are funded solely through a tax imposed on employers, except for three states that also require minimal employee contributions.
- *Health Care Act:* Beginning in 2014, under the Health Care Act the majority of individuals are required to obtain and maintain a certain level of health insurance coverage. If coverage is not provided through an employer, the individual may obtain coverage through various state-level health insurance clearinghouses or "exchanges" that have been developed. Certain states have failed to develop an exchange, and individuals in those states may participate through the federal exchange. Individuals who fail to obtain a minimum level of insurance may be subject to additional taxes.

Other Benefits

Employers may also offer various other types of benefits, such as pretax parking and mass transit plans, legal services, club memberships, employee assistance programs, tuition assistance plans, on-site childcare, relocation plans and severance programs. These benefits should be carefully considered before implementation as they may give rise to issues under the Code and ERISA.

11.2. Pension and Retirement Benefits

Employers may offer qualified and nonqualified retirement plans to their employees. Generally, qualified retirement plans are broad-based whereas nonqualified retirement plans must be limited to a select group of management or highly compensated employees. The Federal government also provides eligible individuals with retirement benefits through the Social Security program.

11.2.1. Qualified Retirement Plans

A qualified plan is a way for employers to provide tax-favored retirement benefits to their employees. An employer with a qualified plan sets aside money for its employees' retirement in exchange for a current income tax deduction (at the time the money is set aside). Moreover, the investment gains on the funds accumulate tax-free. Employees do not pay income tax on the contributions and earnings on those contributions until they actually receive the retirement benefits. Because of these tax advantages, qualified plans are highly regulated under the Code and ERISA and must meet numerous operational and documentary requirements, including annual limits on the amounts that may be contributed. Generally, part-time employees may not be excluded from participation in a qualified retirement plan once the employee has worked either: (i) at least 1,000 hours for the employer in one year; or (ii) at least 500 hours per year in three consecutive years (and have attained age 21).

Qualified retirement plans come in multiple forms: (i) defined benefit plans; (ii) defined contribution plans; and (iii) hybrid plans that are defined benefit plans but have characteristics of defined contribution plans. Typically, all but very small employers will offer some form of qualified retirement plan. Defined contribution plans are currently much more common, although companies in traditional manufacturing industries or with union employees may offer a defined benefit plan.

11.2.2. Defined Benefit Pension Plans

Defined benefit plans are structured to provide a certain benefit at retirement. Often this benefit is expressed as a percentage of pay or a flat dollar amount multiplied by the employee's years of service with the employer. The amount of benefit does not change based on the plan's investment gains and losses. In other words, the employer bears the risk of the investment loss since the employer is obligated to "fund" the fixed benefits. An actuary is required to determine how much the employer must contribute each year to fund the plan; funding requirements are regulated by the Code and ERISA. Payments are generally made when an employee retires on or after retirement age, although payments may begin earlier under certain circumstances. The default form of payment is generally an annuity paid in monthly payments. Annuity payments generally last from the date the employee retires until death. If a participant is married at retirement, benefits are generally required to be paid to the spouse for life, if the spouse survives the participant, unless the participant waived this form of benefit, with the consent of the spouse. Other payment options, such as installments or a lump sum, may be available with spousal consent (if applicable).

11.2.3. Defined Contribution Pension Plans

Under a defined contribution plan, the final pension benefit is not known. In these plans, the employee, the employer or both may contribute to the employee's account. The contribution may either be discretionary or a fixed predictable amount. The annual contributions made to this type of retirement plan are allocated to accounts of the participating employees, and the investment experience of the trust fund, whether positive or negative, affects the account balance. In defined contribution plans, the employees bear the risk of loss (and enjoy the gain on investments). The final pension benefit is based on the value of the total account balance (contributions adjusted for earnings and losses) when the benefit is paid (generally at termination of employment or retirement).

Common forms of defined contribution plans include profit sharing, employee stock ownership plans and 401(k) plans. The 401(k) plan is the prevalent type of defined contribution plan in the U.S. Under a "401(k)" plan (named after the section of the Code that sets forth many of the rules of governance), employees are permitted to reduce their taxable pay by contributing a portion of their compensation to the plan on a pretax basis. Employers that provide 401(k) plans may match a portion of the employees' contributions as an incentive for employees to save for retirement. Generally, the employee is given the discretion to direct the investment of the assets held in his or her plan account by selecting from a menu of investment options established by the employer.

The SECURE 2.0 Act of 2022 (SECURE 2.0) was passed in December 2022, providing comprehensive updates and changes that affect employer-sponsored defined contribution plans. Under SECURE 2.0, beginning on or after January 1, 2025, employers of almost all *new* defined contribution plans will be required to auto-enroll employees upon hire (existing plans are exempt from this provision). SECURE 2.0 also provides employers with the option to provide for automatic enrollment in current 401(k) and 403(b) plans. However, SECURE 2.0 mandates employers to automatically enroll all eligible employees in *new* 401(k) and 403(b) plans (i.e., those plans beginning after December 31, 2024) at a new default rate and to automatically escalate participants' deferral rate each year, up to a maximum of 15%, with some exceptions for new and small businesses. An exception to this requirement is when the employee elects to opt out. Moreover, effective December 31, 2023, a defined contribution plan permits participants who have attained age 50 to make catch-up contributions, the catch-up contributions are required to be made on a Roth basis for participants who earn at least USD 145,000.00 or more in the prior year. Additionally, under SECURE 2.0, if an employer chooses to make 401(k) contributions to part-time employees, employers may match a portion of part-time employees' contributions who worked at least 500 hours in a twelve-month period for two consecutive years. However, this two-year provision does not take effect until January 1, 2025, meaning the original three-year provision still applies up until December 31, 2024. Employers should start tracking hours for part-time employees to determine whether they will be eligible in 2024 or 2025 under this provision.

11.2.4. Governmental Retirement Benefits

Social Security is a social insurance program funded by payroll taxes, which are shared by the employer and its employees. Under this program, the Federal government makes retirement benefits available to employees, and these benefits are administered by the Social Security Administration (SSA), an independent agency of the Federal government. An employee's retirement income is generally based on the average of the highest thirty-five years of the employee's covered earnings and is calculated after taking a number of factors into account. Retirement income will normally begin being paid out on a monthly basis at a retiree's normal retirement age (age 65, 66 or 67, depending on the employee's year of birth).

11.2.5. Executive Compensation

Employers may offer a variety of compensation programs to their executives, including deferred compensation plans, severance programs, bonus programs and change-in-control benefits. Although many of these arrangements are negotiated and covered by general contract principles, care should be taken to ensure the arrangements also comply with the Code, as well as with ERISA, if applicable.

11.2.6. Nonqualified Retirement Plans

Nonqualified retirement plans are often used to compensate highly paid employees and executives because the limits on the benefits and contributions that can be provided under qualified retirement plans are too low to sustain the executive's standard of living at retirement. When nonqualified retirement plans operate in conjunction with qualified retirement plans, they may be called "supplemental" plans, supplemental employee retirement plans, "excess" plans, "wrap" plans or "mirror" plans.

Nonqualified retirement plans are not subject to the benefit and contribution limits imposed on qualified plans under the Code and ERISA but may be subject to other requirements of the Code and ERISA. In general, if a nonqualified retirement plan is properly drafted and administered, participants will not be taxed on their benefit until receipt.

Unlike qualified plans whose assets are protected in a trust, a nonqualified retirement plan must be unfunded or have its assets held in a special "rabbi" trust, which is subject to the claims of the employer's general creditors. This means that participants do not receive any priority over the employer's other creditors in the event of the employer's insolvency, even though they may have made contributions of their own money to the nonqualified retirement plan. In other words, nonqualified plan participants have only unsecured claims for their benefits.

11.2.7. Code Section 409A Compliance

Nonqualified deferred compensation plans must comply with the documentation and operational requirements of Code section 409A, unless otherwise exempt. The definition of deferred compensation is broad and can encompass any arrangement that provides an employee with a legally binding right during a taxable year to compensation that is or may become payable in a later taxable year. Code section 409A is complex, and the failure to comply with Code section 409A will accelerate the taxation of the deferred payment and impose a significant additional federal income (penalty) tax (20%) and premium interest tax on the employee. Although the cost of noncompliance falls primarily on the employee, there are also consequences for the employer, including tax reporting and withholding obligations.

11.2.8. Code Section 457A Compliance

Under Code section 457A, deferred compensation received by a U.S. taxpayer under a nonqualified deferred compensation arrangement sponsored by a nonqualified entity is includible in taxable income when the deferred amount is no longer subject to a substantial risk of forfeiture (generally, when the deferred amount "vests"). A nonqualified entity includes any non-U.S. company unless substantially all of its income is either: (i) effectively connected with a U.S. trade or business or (ii) subject to a comprehensive income tax outside the U.S. The failure to comply with Code section 457A will accelerate the taxation of the deferred payment and impose a significant additional federal income (penalty) tax (20%) and premium interest tax on the employee.

11.2.9. Equity Compensation Arrangements

An employer may use its equity to compensate its employees. Equity compensation is generally subject to tax laws, securities laws and state corporate laws in the U.S.; however, equity compensation is generally exempt from ERISA.

11.2.10. Stock Options

An employer may grant employees the option to purchase its stock under a stock option plan. These grants may be broad-based or targeted to key employees. Options may be tax-advantaged Incentive Stock Options (ISOs) or Nonqualified Stock Options (NSOs). The recipient of an NSO is generally subject to income tax on the spread at the time the NSO is exercised. The recipient of an ISO is generally not taxed on the spread at exercise, assuming certain holding and other requirements are met, but is subject to tax, at capital gains rates, on the subsequent appreciation in the value of the option shares when he disposes of such shares. To avoid the potential application of Code section 409A, stock options must generally be granted with an exercise price equal to the fair market value of the underlying stock on the date of grant.

11.2.11. Employee Stock Purchase Plans

Employers may offer their employees a stock purchase plan (ESPP). If the ESPP is a broad-based program designed to comply with Code section 423, then the employees may be offered the shares at a discount with favorable tax treatment. In addition, if certain holding period requirements are satisfied, the employee is taxed at ordinary income tax rates on the spread between the purchase price and the fair market value of the underlying stock on the date of grant and any additional gain will be taxed at capital gain rates. These plans typically permit employees to purchase shares on regular purchase dates using payroll deductions to accumulate the funds for the purchase price.

11.2.12. Other Stock-Based Compensation

Other forms of stock-based compensation include restricted stock, restricted stock units, phantom shares and Stock Appreciation Rights (SARs). Restricted stock is generally subject to income tax at vesting. The income tax event for restricted stock units is after vesting upon delivery of the underlying shares (or the cash value thereof). Phantom shares and SARs are not actual equity awards (unless the SAR is a stock-settled SAR), but rather use the stock value on the date of grant as a measure of the amount of the award. An employee exercising an SAR or cashing out a phantom share is generally entitled to the appreciation in the value of the shares since grant. The award can be paid in cash or stock and is taxed as ordinary income. As with options, to avoid the potential application of Code section 409A, SARs must generally be granted with an exercise price equal to the fair market value of the underlying stock on the date of grant.

11.3. Payment of Benefits on Termination

Whether accrued but unused vacation must be paid to an employee, who is terminated is governed by state law. In some states, employers may be required to pay out an employee's accrued vacation upon termination of employment, and annual "use it or lose it" vacation policies may not be permissible. In other states, a company's payout of accrued vacation is regulated by company policy. In general, employers are not required to pay holiday pay at termination. "Floating" holidays, which may be taken at the employee's discretion, may be required to be treated like vacation, however, and be paid out according to the applicable state law.

11.3.1. Checklist

- Employers in the U.S. should confirm that employee retirement and medical plans meet the requirements of ERISA and the Code, to the extent applicable, as well as any other applicable federal or state law. Failure to comply with such requirements may result in adverse tax consequences for the employer or the employee.
- Employers should also confirm that any nonqualified deferred compensation arrangements are either exempt from or compliant with the requirements of Code section 409A and Code section 457A. Failure to comply with such laws may result in an additional federal income (penalty) tax (20%) and premium interest tax on the employee.

11.4. Leaves of Absence

11.4.1. Personal Leave

U.S. Federal law does not require companies to pay employees for any type of personal leave. Exempt salaried employees, however, may need to be paid for partial-day absences due to personal reasons, sickness or disability if they perform some work during the workweek. The length of, and any compensation, and benefits paid during a personal leave, is a matter of agreement between an employer and an employee (or the employee's representative).

11.4.2. Medical or Sick Leave

The Family and Medical Leave Act (FMLA) requires that: (i) private employers with fifty or more employees; and (ii) public employers must provide eligible employees up to twelve workweeks of unpaid leave in a twelve-month period for the birth of a child, the serious health condition of the employee or to care for an immediate family member. Eligible employees are those who work at a facility with fifty or more employees within a 75-mile radius, have more than twelve months of service with the employer, and who have worked at least 1,250 hours during the previous twelve-month period before the date the leave begins.

Federal law does not require the employer to pay employees for any time off during the leave period, although some employers do so voluntarily, and some state and local laws require pay for time off. The employer must, however, continue to provide the employee coverage under its group health plan during the leave period as if the employee was working his or her regular schedule. Yet, there is currently a trend for states and localities—including New York, California, Massachusetts, the District of Columbia, Chicago, Illinois, Maryland, Delaware, and Maine—to enact laws, or add to those already existing, that require paid sick, medical, and/or family leave. Employers should refer to their state requirements for paid leave.

If the sickness or illness is a qualifying "disability" under the Americans with Disabilities Act (ADA), the employer may also be required to provide reasonable accommodations to the employee to allow the employee to continue to work. Such accommodation may include a different job or work schedule, job duties or a leave of absence (although not unlimited in duration). All businesses that have fifteen or more employees must comply with the ADA.

It is important to note, however, that some state laws and city or county ordinances may also require greater or longer medical or sick leave for employees.

11.4.3. Bereavement Leave

Federal law does not require bereavement leave. Many employers, however, voluntarily provide paid bereavement leave to their employees.

11.4.4. Family Leave

The FMLA requires that covered employers must provide an eligible employee up to a total of twelve workweeks of unpaid leave during any twelve-month period for one or more of the following reasons: (i) the birth and care of a newborn child of the employee; (ii) the placement and care of a newly-placed adoptive or foster care child with the employee; (iii) care for an immediate family member (spouse, child or parent) with a serious health condition; (iv) leave if the employee is unable to work because of a serious health condition; or (v) a qualifying exigency arising out of the employee's immediate family member being a military member on covered active duty status (or notice of an impending call or order to covered active duty).

The FMLA also provides leave for employees with families of military including: (i) up to twenty-six weeks of leave in a single twelve-month period to care for an injured service member; and (ii) up to twelve weeks of leave in a twelve-month period due to any "qualifying exigency" because a family member has been called to active duty.

More and more states and cities or counties are now requiring employers to provide some type of "paid" family leave for employees and may apply to smaller employers. Some state and local laws require leave for a broader universe of circumstances. For example, any additional leave benefits are generally a matter of agreement between an employer and an employee.

11.4.5. Pregnancy Leave/Maternity Leave

The FMLA requires employers to provide unpaid leave for pregnancy. This leave can be used for prenatal care appointments and any period of incapacity, including morning sickness, and for "baby bonding" after the child is born. If the pregnancy results in health complications that rise to the level of a "disability," the employer may need to consider additional leave under the ADA as a "reasonable accommodation."

Several states and municipalities also require employers to provide pregnancy and/or maternity leave and some state laws apply to smaller employers. Any further leave benefits are generally a matter of agreement between an employer and an employee.

11.4.6. Injury at Work

When employees are injured on the job that results in a "serious health condition" or "disability," they may be entitled to medical and/or disability-related leave under the FMLA or the ADA. In addition, state workers' compensation laws require that some compensation and benefits be paid to the injured employee. Companies may also have their own policies that provide leave or other benefits to employees injured on the job (*see also* section 12).

12. WORKERS' COMPENSATION

State workers' compensation laws provide payments to workers who are injured on their jobs. Workers' compensation laws also provide monetary benefits to the family of workers who are killed or injured during the course of their employment either from accidents or illnesses.

Although most states have their own workers' compensation statutes which apply to private sector employees, the Federal Employment Compensation

Act provides workers' compensation for federal civilian employees. The Federal Employers' Liability Act provides coverage to employees of interstate railroads or of any common carrier by railroad while engaging in commerce between any of the states.

12.1. State Laws

There is generally no federal law of workers' compensation for injured employees of private companies. Rather, individual states have specific laws which require that an employer compensate injured employees who cannot work as a result of job-related injury or illness. These laws also require employers to pay for necessary and reasonable medical expenses. In some states, job-related injury or illness may include mental injuries and stress in addition to physical injuries. These state laws generally provide an employee's exclusive remedy for workplace injuries and they give employers immunity from paying unlimited damages in tort or negligence lawsuits, although in some instances the employer may still face intentional tort liability. Workers' compensation laws may not cover some small employers, domestic employees, agricultural workers, casual workers or independent contractors.

All states require employers to carry either workers' compensation insurance, self-insurance or participate in the state's workers' compensation fund. If an employer does not have one of these coverages, the injured employee may be able to sue the employer directly. In some states, failure to comply with workers' compensation insurance requirements subjects the employer to potential criminal and civil penalties. Employers that carry workers' compensation insurance should confirm that any coverage is consistent with the requirements of the Federal Affordable Care Act.

12.2. Defenses to Claims of Compensation

It is difficult for an employer to deny a claim for workers' compensation because it is generally a "no fault" system. Even if an employee is negligent or reckless, the employee may still be entitled to compensation. In most cases, even a violation of the employer's rules or procedures will not relieve the employer from its duty to compensate an injured employee, unless the violation is so egregious that it removes the employee from the scope of employment when the accident occurred.

An employee is not eligible for compensation if he or she is injured during the commission of a criminal act or during the commission of or an attempted suicide. In these situations, the "accident" did not arise out of the course of employment but rather from the employee's own personal motivations.

12.3. Other

Although state worker's compensation laws generally stop an employee from suing the employer for negligence, the employee may still sue a third party, such as the manufacturer of a machine which caused the injury or a product or material which caused injury to the employee's health.

13. LAWS PERTAINING TO WORKPLACE SAFETY

13.1. Overview

Workplace safety in the U.S. is regulated by both federal and state laws. The primary federal law is the Occupational Safety and Health Act (OSHA) which sets rules and regulations pertaining to workplace inspections and the imposition of penalties. The U.S. DOL enforces the increasingly complex OSHA standards by more aggressive assessment of penalties, inspections and possible criminal liability for willful violations of OSHA.

Most states also have some type of laws that also protect workers and may cover workplace hazards not included under OSHA.

13.2. Federal Rules and Regulations

OSHA requires a covered employer to: (i) provide employees with safety training programs and information regarding the safety considerations associated with the various components of their jobs; (ii) maintain a workplace free of hazards; and (iii) maintain accurate records of work-related injuries and illnesses or work-related deaths.

An employee has the right to file a complaint with OSHA as well as his or her employer of any possible workplace hazards. It is unlawful for an employer to take any action or "retaliate" against an employee who files a complaint.

13.3. Workplace Injuries/Records

As a general rule, employers with more than ten employees (unless otherwise exempt) must maintain reports (OSHA Forms 300, 300A and 301) and records of all work-related injuries and illnesses resulting in death, absence from work, work restrictions, transfer to another job, medical treatment beyond first aid and/or unconsciousness (OSHA Form 300).

13.4. Potential Violence in the Workplace

Potential workplace violence is recognized as workplace safety and health hazard in the U.S. Accordingly, employers are legally obligated to prevent workplace violence and are subject to citation for failure to implement proper workplace violence policies.

All employers, regardless of size, should have some type of workplace violence policy or procedure which provides, in part: (i) a statement that the employer will not tolerate any physical and verbal acts or threats of violence, harassment or bullying and any employee committing violent acts or threats will be disciplined; (ii) a request that an employee must notify the employer about actual or threatened violent acts or threats; (iii) a statement that the employer will immediately investigate any actual or threatened violent acts or threats of violence; (iv) a statement that the employer will impose appropriate discipline for violations of its workplace violence policy and procedures.

13.5. Fines and Penalties

Failure to comply with applicable OSHA rules, regulations and standards may expose an employer to significant penalties, fines, litigation and civil liability. Employers and individual company representatives may also be subject to criminal prosecution for willful violations of OSHA and prosecuted under state laws.

14. IMMIGRATION, SECONDMENT AND FOREIGN ASSIGNMENT

14.1. Overview of Law Controlling Immigration

The federal statute governing U.S. immigration law and policy is the Immigration and Nationality Act (INA). The INA sets forth the structure of the U.S. immigration system, including: (i) a preference system for allocating immigrant visas based on skills and family relationships; (ii) a process for becoming a naturalized citizen of the U.S.; (iii) controls for admitting both immigrants and nonimmigrants to the U.S., including foreign workers; (iv) grounds for excluding and removing non-U.S. citizens from the U.S.; and (v) penalties for violating immigration laws, including the unlawful employment of aliens and unfair immigration-related employment practices.

The INA has been amended several times through the enactment of public laws. Some of the most significant amendments impacting the employment of foreign workers are: (i) the Immigration Reform and Control Act of 1986 (IRCA), which required employers to verify the employment eligibility of all employees and imposed penalties for failing to do so; (ii) the Immigration Act of 1990 (IMMACT90), which set the current annual quotas for employment-based immigrants and created new immigrant and nonimmigrant visa categories for foreign workers; (iii) the American Competitiveness in the Twenty-First Century Act (AC21), which addressed issues relating to the admission of highly skilled workers to the U.S.; and (iv) the PATRIOT Act, which required the development of better controls and systems for tracking individuals entering the U.S.

U.S. immigration laws are implemented and enforced by three key federal agencies: the Department of Homeland Security (DHS), the Department of State (DOS) and the DOL. DHS has developed separate internal agencies for adjudicating immigration benefits, admitting individuals at the border, and investigating immigration violations. These internal agencies include U.S. Citizenship and Immigration Services (USCIS), U.S. Customs and Border Protection (CBP), and U.S. Immigration and Customs Enforcement (ICE). The immigration regulations promulgated by all of these federal agencies are contained in sections 8, 20 and 22 of the Code of Federal Regulations.

14.2. Recruiting, Screening and Hiring Process

The INA's antidiscrimination provisions prohibit employers from discriminating against certain protected classes with respect to hiring, recruiting, and discharging from employment because of national origin or citizenship status.

The national origin discrimination provisions contained in the INA apply to all persons who are currently authorized to work in the U.S. In contrast, the citizenship status discrimination provisions only apply to U.S. citizens, lawful permanent residents, temporary residents, asylees and refugees. This means that most nonimmigrants (e.g., H-1B or L-1 visa holders) are not covered by the citizenship status discrimination provisions.

Although a finding of discrimination under U.S. immigration law requires a finding of the employer's discriminatory intent which can be a difficult burden to meet, employers should not disregard the importance of these antidiscrimination provisions. Activities such as specifying documents that an employee must present to verify employment eligibility in the context of an offer letter or during the verification process or inquiring about an applicant's immigration status on a job application or during an interview, can give rise to discrimination claims. Employers may face civil fines and other penalties for committing unfair immigration-related employment practices.

Title VII of the Civil Rights Act of 1964 also contains a national origin discrimination provision that protects persons regardless of employment authorization status. Therefore, potential national origin discrimination claims should be analyzed from both an immigration and employment law perspective.

14.3. Obligation of an Employer to Enforce Immigration Laws

Employers are required to verify the employment eligibility of all employees hired on or after November 7, 1986, by completing the I-9 (Employment Eligibility Verification) Form. At the time of hire, the employee must attest, under penalty of perjury, that he or she is authorized to work in the U.S. as a U.S. citizen, a noncitizen national of the U.S., a lawful permanent resident, or a nonimmigrant with a time-limited form of work authorization. At the time of hire, the employee must also present original documents to establish identity and employment authorization. Within three days of hire, the employer must review the original documents and record the relevant information (i.e., type of document, document number and expiration date, if any) on the I-9 Form. If the employee provides a document expiration date in the employee's section of the I-9 Form, the employer also must reverify the employee's employment eligibility before that date has passed. The employer must retain the completed I-9 Form for at least three years from the date of hire, or one year after employment terminates, whichever is later.

DHS currently offers two programs to assist employers in complying with the employment eligibility verification requirements: E-Verify and IMAGE (ICE Mutual Agreement between Government and Employers).

E-Verify is an online system operated jointly by DHS and the SSA. Participating employers must check the work authorization status of new hires online by comparing information from the person's I-9 Form against DHS and SSA databases. E-Verify is a voluntary program for most employers. However, some states require the use of E-Verify. Additionally, E-Verify is mandatory for employers with federal contracts or subcontracts that contain the Federal Acquisition Regulation E-Verify clause.

The IMAGE program is another voluntary program that is designed to assist employers in targeted sectors to reduce unauthorized employment and prevent the use of fraudulent identity documents by employees. Employers participating in the IMAGE program must enroll in E-Verify, undergo an I-9 audit conducted by ICE, and adhere to ICE's "Best Employment Practices" which includes the development of a self-reporting procedure to notify ICE of any violations.

14.4. Fines and Penalties

Employers that do not accurately complete and retain I-9 Forms may face civil fines of up to USD 2,507.00 for each "paperwork" violation and up to USD 2,322.00 for second and subsequent offenses. The severity of the penalty will be determined by: (i) the size of the business; (ii) the employer's good faith efforts to comply with the law; (iii) the number of unauthorized employees; and (iv) whether the employer has a history of violations. Employers that have technical or procedural errors in their I-9 records may be considered to be in compliance if they have otherwise made a good faith attempt to comply with the employment verification requirements.

Employers that knowingly hire unauthorized workers may face civil sanctions of up to USD 5,016.00 per unauthorized worker for an employer's first offense. Additionally, employers that engage in a "pattern or practice" of employing unauthorized workers may face civil sanctions of up to USD 27,018.00 as well as criminal fines of up to USD 3,000.00 for each unauthorized worker, and the responsible executive or manager who condones the practice may be imprisoned for up to six months. Employers may also be fined under Title 18 of the United States Code, or imprisoned for up to five years, or both, for knowingly hiring ten or more unauthorized workers during a twelve-month period.

Employers are liable for both actual and "constructive" knowledge that an employee is not authorized to work. Constructive knowledge can be imputed to an employer for failing to respond to a "No-Match" letter from the SSA, indicating that an employee's name and social security number on Form W-2 do not match SSA records. Thus, employers that receive such letters are prudent to check their records, inform the employee of the discrepancy, and give the employee a reasonable amount of time to resolve the problem with SSA.

Furthermore, an employer can face criminal penalties for failing to disclose its role as a document preparer when sponsoring an employee for immigration benefits. Specifically, a person who knowingly fails to disclose, conceal or cover up the fact that they have assisted in preparing a falsely made application for immigration benefits may be fined under Title 18 of the United States Code, imprisoned for up to five years, or both. Thus, it is imperative that all documents filed by employers to procure immigration benefits for current or prospective employees should be thoroughly reviewed and signed only after careful scrutiny.

14.5. Secondment/Foreign Assignment

Employers seeking to second, transfer or hire a foreign worker in the U.S. must typically sponsor the worker for nonimmigrant (temporary) or immigrant (permanent) work authorization. The work authorization must be secured before the foreign worker can commence employment in the U.S. To obtain work authorization for a foreign worker, the U.S. employer must file a petition with USCIS or, in some cases, directly at a U.S. port-of-entry or U.S. Consulate abroad. The purpose of the petition is to confirm that the foreign worker has the specific education, experience or skills to qualify for the particular type of work authorization.

The U.S. visa system includes a variety of visa options. However, quota limitations can impact certain categories, in particular the H category for specialty occupation professionals. In addition, the expectations of the U.S. immigration agencies for proof of eligibility vary at different times.

To determine the type of employment authorization appropriate for an executive or business professional, it is necessary to examine:

- the nature of the work to be performed in the U.S.;
- the expected length of stay;
- the person's educational and professional credentials;
- the employer's long-term business plans.

Among the types of nonimmigrant visas available for executives and business professionals are:

- B (for business and pleasure visitors);
- E (for treaty traders, treaty investors, and Australian citizens in specialty occupations);
- H (for temporary trainees or professional workers);
- J (for exchange visitors, including corporate trainees);
- L (for intracompany transferees);
- O (for aliens of extraordinary ability in the sciences, arts, education, business or athletics, or with a record of extraordinary achievement in the motion picture or television industry, and accompanying aliens providing essential support);
- TN (for Canadian or Mexican business persons entering the U.S. pursuant to the work authorization provisions of the North American Free Trade Agreement (NAFTA)).

These visas vary in terms of purpose, eligibility, permitted length of U.S. stay and renewability. Additionally, all of these nonimmigrant visa categories, except the B category, provide for the issuance of dependent visas to the spouse and minor children of the nonimmigrant visa holder so that they may accompany the employee during the U.S. assignment. The E, L and, in limited circumstances, the H-1B visa categories also allow the accompanying spouse to obtain work authorization. The other categories typically do not provide work authorization for accompanying spouses.

There are five employment-based immigrant visa preference categories under which a person may qualify for U.S. permanent resident status (i.e., a "green card"). The first employment-based preference category includes aliens of extraordinary ability, outstanding professors and researchers, and certain multinational managers and executives. The second preference employment-based category includes members of the professions who hold advanced degrees, or because of their exceptional ability in the sciences, arts or business, will substantially benefit the national economy, cultural or educational interests or the welfare of the U.S. The third preference category includes professionals, skilled workers and other workers. The fourth and fifth preference categories provide immigrant visas for special immigrants (religious workers, among others) and investors who make investments of USD 800,000.00–USD 1,050,000.00 or more and create at least ten full-time jobs, respectively.

The most appropriate preference category for a person largely depends on the requirements for the position sought in the U.S., and the person's education and experience. A person's citizenship can also play an important factor in developing a permanent residence strategy. A limited number of green cards are allocated to applicants in a particular preference category from each country per year. The quota for each preference category is filled on a first-come, first-served basis. Therefore, persons within certain categories from countries with high U.S. immigration rates may experience longer delays during the application process.

The procedure for obtaining a green card based on employment generally involves three steps: filing a Labor Certification or "PERM" application with the DOL, after testing the labor market to verify that there are no qualified and interested U.S. workers for the position offered; filing the Form I-140, Immigrant Petition, with the USCIS to request that the person be found qualified for U.S. permanent residence; and filing the Form I-485, Application to Adjust Status, or Form DS-230, Application for an Immigrant Visa, to confirm that the person and his or her accompanying family members meet the minimum health, financial and government-determined moral standards for obtaining U.S. permanent resident status.

Employers may bypass the PERM application process and immediately proceed with the Immigrant Petition if their foreign national employee can qualify in one of the first preference, employment-based immigrant visa categories. Additionally, if the applicant is not subject to a quota-based backlog, the Application to Adjust Status can be submitted to the USCIS concurrently with the Immigrant Petition.

When adjudicating requests for both temporary and permanent work authorization, DHS and/or DOS will conduct a criminal background check of the foreign worker. Foreign workers with certain types of criminal convictions will need to obtain special permission to enter the U.S. for a work assignment. If the criminal offense is serious enough, the foreign worker may be precluded from entering the U.S. Additionally, DHS and/or DOS will request information about a foreign worker's health history when processing requests for work authorization. Medical examinations are not typically required to process requests for temporary work authorization; however, they are mandatory for permanent work authorization.

14.6. Checklist

- Employers should implement a comprehensive immigration compliance program and review existing immigration and employment policies, as well as immigration-related provisions of standard employment applications and offer letters, to ensure compliance with U.S. immigration law.
- Employers should provide ongoing training to all personnel involved in the hiring process regarding the appropriate procedures for completing, reverifying and retaining I-9 Forms, and the appropriate ways to ask questions about a job candidate's U.S. immigration status.
- Employers should conduct regular I-9 audits and take corrective measures as necessary.
- Employers should develop a management system to obtain the required visa and work authorization for foreign workers, and to monitor the visa and work permit renewal needs for each such worker.
- Employers should carefully review all petitions and applications for immigration benefits before submission to a government agency.

15. RESTRICTIVE COVENANTS AND PROTECTION OF TRADE SECRETS AND CONFIDENTIAL INFORMATION

15.1. Overview

After an employee is terminated from his or her employment, the employee is generally free to work for a former employer's competitor and to use his or her general skills and knowledge at a new job unless otherwise restricted by contract.

An employee may not, however, use or disclose a former employer's "trade secrets." Employers in the U.S. are increasingly concerned about the protection of business "trade secrets." Technology in the workplace has made trade secret misappropriation easier because valuable trade secret information may be readily transferred using computers, portable storage devices and other digital media. In addition, increasing employee mobility has yielded greater opportunities for employees to take trade secrets to their new employers.

To best protect a company's trade secrets, it is common for employers to require employees to sign confidentiality agreements prohibiting the use and disclosure of confidential and trade secret information. It is also common for employers to restrict employees from working for a competitor and soliciting coworkers and/or customers for a limited period of time following the termination of employment. These agreements are commonly referred to as "noncompete" agreements or "restrictive covenants." Employers often require key employees to agree to restrictive covenants in order to protect the employer's confidential and trade secret information and/or the employer's important customer relationships. Restrictive covenants are generally controlled by state law and are generally enforceable in most states, provided their terms are narrowly tailored to protect these legitimate employer interests rather than simply restrict otherwise legal competition.

15.2. The Law of Trade Secrets

"Trade secrets" are legally protected under state law in every jurisdiction, as well as under federal law. The Defend Trade Secrets Act (DTSA), enacted in May 2016, created a federal civil cause of action for trade secret misappropriation for trade secrets which are "related to a product or service used in, intended for use in, interstate or foreign commerce."[4] The Act broadly defines a "trade secret" to include both technical and non-technical information, including "programs" and "codes," which:

(i) is the subject of reasonable secrecy measures taken by the trade secret owner; and

(ii) derives "independent economic value, actual or potential, from not being generally known to, and not being readily ascertainable through proper means by, another person who can obtain economic value from the disclosure or use of the information."[5]

4. 18 USC § 1836(b)(1).
5. 18 USC § 1839(3).

Examples of trade secrets include: manufacturing processes, product formulas, customer lists, business plans and strategies and financial information. As a general rule, a claim by an employer that its information is a trade secret will be tested with the following inquiries: (i) a demand for specific identification of the secret(s) in question; (ii) a demand for documents and information showing that the employer actually owns the trade secret(s); and (iii) a demand for evidence that the trade secret(s) has been adequately guarded and has in fact been kept secret, i.e., not published in some way through other leak points.

Under the DTSA, a trade secret is "misappropriated" if it is:

(i) acquired "by a person who knows or has reason to know that the trade secret was acquired by improper means" ("improper means" is defined to include "theft, bribery, misrepresentation, breach or inducement of a breach of a duty to maintain secrecy, or espionage through electronic or other means"); or
(ii) disclosed or used by a person who:
  (a) "used improper means to acquire knowledge of the trade secret";
  (b) "at the time of disclosure or use knew or had reason to know that the knowledge of the trade secret was" (1) derived from or through a person who had used improper means to acquire the trade secret; (2) acquired under circumstances giving rise to a duty to maintain the secrecy of the trade secret or limit its use; or (3) derived from a person who owed a duty to maintain the secrecy of the trade secret or limit its use; or
  (c) "before a material change of position of the person, knew or had reason to know that" (1) the trade secret was a "trade secret"; and (2) knowledge of the trade secret had been acquired by accident or mistake.[6]

In summary, to establish misappropriation, at the very least an employer must prove that the wrongdoer knew or had reason to know that the person or entity from whom it received the trade secret in question obtained the trade secret by improper means.

Under the DTSA, "actual or threatened" misappropriation of the Company's trade secret may also be enjoined, and the defendant may be ordered to take "affirmative" steps to protect the Company's trade secret.[7] The Company could recover damages for actual loss, a defendant's wrongful gains and exemplary damages.[8] Significantly, the DTSA also permits ex

6. 18 USC § 1839(5).
7. 18 USC § 1836(b)(3)(A).
8. *Ibid.*

parte civil seizure orders "in extraordinary circumstances" where a seizure of the property embodying the trade secret is "necessary to prevent its propagation or dissemination."[9] However, the search and seizure remedy is available only where it "clearly appears from the specific facts" that a defendant would "evade, avoid or otherwise refuse to comply with" an injunction order prohibiting the use or disclosure of the trade secret.[10]

Trade secrets are also protected under state law. While some states still apply common law trade secret principles, most states have also adopted some version of the multijurisdictional model law known as the Uniform Trade Secrets Act (UTSA). The UTSA defines "trade secret" in substantially the same manner as the federal DTSA. In addition, in most states, the actual or threatened misappropriation of trade secret information may be enjoined by a court. Under the UTSA, courts are also empowered to award compensatory and punitive damages for trade secret misappropriation, as well as attorneys' fees to the prevailing party when it is determined that misappropriation is willful. Under limited circumstances, many states also recognize the doctrine of "inevitable" trade secret misappropriation. "Inevitable" trade secret misappropriation is based on the theory that under some circumstances, a former employee is unable to separate knowledge of a former employer's trade secrets from the performance of his new job responsibilities with a competing employer. In those circumstances, courts may stop a former employee from engaging in competitive activities at his new employment, even in the absence of evidence of actual or threatened trade secret theft.

Trade secrets are also protected under a federal criminal statute known as the Economic Espionage Act (the "EEA") (18 U.S.C. §§ 1831 et seq.). The EEA imposes criminal penalties for two distinct but related types of trade secret misappropriations: (i) "economic espionage" (18 U.S.C. § 1831); and (ii) theft of trade secrets (28 U.S.C. § 1832).

Under section 1831, it is a crime to knowingly steal or misappropriate a trade secret to "benefit any foreign government, foreign instrumentality or foreign agent."[11] A "foreign instrumentality" is an entity that is dominated or controlled by a foreign government.[12] An individual violating section 1831 of the EEA may be fined in an amount not exceeding USD 5,000,000.00 and/or imprisoned for not more than fifteen years.[13]

Section 1832 of the EEA makes it a crime to knowingly steal or misappropriate a trade secret benefiting anyone other than the trade secret's owner. Unlike section 1831, section 1832 does not require proof of a nexus

9. 18 USC § 1836(b)(2).
10. *Ibid.*
11. 18 U.S.C. § 1831(a).
12. 18 U.S.C. § 1839(1).
13. 28 U.S.C. § 1831(a)(5).

to a foreign government. The following elements in section 1832 are also not present in section 1831: (i) the defendant must intend an economic benefit to someone other than the trade secret owner; (ii) the trade secret must be "related to a product or service used in or intended for use in" commerce; and (iii) the defendant must know that the conduct would injure the trade secret owner.[14] Section 1832 provides for imprisonment of up to ten years and/or a monetary penalty not to exceed the greater of USD 5,000,000.00 or three times "the value of the stolen trade secret to the organization, including expenses for research and design and other costs of reproducing the trade secret."

15.3. Restrictive Covenants and Noncompete Agreements

Restrictive covenants are contractual restraints on competition that may include: (i) covenants preventing an employee from going to work for a competitor in any capacity for a limited time period following termination; (ii) covenants preventing an employee from soliciting customers for a limited time period following termination; (iii) covenants preventing an employee from soliciting employees of the former employer for a limited time period following termination; and (iv) provisions in benefit plans that would cause a former employee to forfeit future compensation or benefits, such as stock options, in the event of competition.

The particular rules governing the enforcement of restrictive covenants vary from state to state. Some states, such as California, do not allow for the enforcement of employee post-termination noncompete agreements as a matter of public policy. Other states, such as Massachusetts, may require employers to compensate employees during the post-employment restricted period.

In determining whether to enforce an employee restrictive covenant, most state courts follow the "rule of reasonableness." Under this approach, a restrictive covenant will be enforced if an employer's legitimate proprietary interest needs protection, and the covenant is reasonably limited in terms of subject matter, duration and geographic scope. The court determines whether the time, subject matter and territorial limitation imposed by the covenant have reasonable relationship to an employer's legitimate proprietary interest. An employer's "legitimate proprietary interests" generally consist of the protection of confidential and trade secret information and the protection of customer relationships.

14. 18 U.S.C. § 1832(a).

Time, territory and subject matter limitations should be consistent with the scope of employer's proprietary interests in its customer relationships and/or confidential information and the employee's actual activities during employment. For example, if an employer's only protectable interest is its customer relationships, a customer non-solicitation covenant is more appropriate than a covenant completely barring any form of competition. Similarly, if an employer's trade secrets have a short "shelf life," the duration of the covenant should not exceed the "shelf life" of the secrets.

Employers should be aware that, at this time, the Federal Trade Commission (FTC) has proposed and extended the public comment period for a new rule to challenge the current noncompete law and ban employers from imposing noncompetes on their workers altogether, based on a preliminary finding that noncompetes constitute an unfair method of competition and therefore violate section 5 of the Federal Trade Commission Act. As pro-business groups have publicly announced their intention to challenge the proposed noncompete ban, we anticipate that this will be stayed subject to further litigation in federal court.

16. "WHISTLEBLOWER" PROTECTION

16.1. Overview

Both federal and state laws in the U.S. provide some type of protection for "whistleblower" employees who oppose or report unlawful activities of their employers. These protections may extend to employees who oppose unsafe workplace conditions, discriminatory or harassing conduct in the workplace (*see* section 17.4.3), anti-union practices or illegal immigration practices. The Dodd-Frank and Sarbanes-Oxley laws also protect employees who report financial fraud or inadequate or inaccurate corporate books and records. Other statutes protect employees for opposing practices impacting the public at large, such as product safety, anticompetitive/antitrust practices, environmental or tax violations. These "whistleblower" laws protect employees from retaliatory adverse employment actions. Some laws also "reward" employees with a "bounty" or monetary share of the government's recovery for illegal activities.

In addition to federal laws, many states also protect employees who report or threaten to report a violation to a governmental entity, participate in a government investigation, hearing or inquiry, oppose or refuse to participate in unlawful conduct, or participate in an internal employer investigation.

Some states allow employees to bring not only contractual claims but also a tort claim for wrongful discharge in violation of public policy.

Most "whistleblower" laws protect employees from adverse employment action if the employee in good faith believed that there was a violation of a law. The employee would not need to prove that the underlying alleged activity actually occurred or was actually unlawful. Whistleblower statutes do require, however, that the employee prove some causal connection between the complaint and the adverse employment action.

If a company retaliates against a whistleblowing employee, the employee may be entitled to reinstatement to the same or equivalent job and compensation for lost pay and benefits. Some states may also allow recovery of monies for emotional distress, attorneys' fees and punitive damages for the tort of wrongful discharge.

16.2. Checklist

- Employers should always investigate formal or informal complaints by employees as soon as possible and document their resolution.
- Companies should issue a "litigation hold" notice (requiring all of its employees to preserve all data that may relate to any legal action) immediately upon notice of threatened litigation, government investigation or administrative procedure.
- Managers and supervisors should be trained to recognize and report any complaints of unlawful conduct, workplace discrimination, or possible corporate compliance or ethical violations to the appropriate representatives in the company.
- Managers, supervisors and representatives of human resources should be trained to manage employee discipline and terminations carefully if they involve a possible "whistleblower," and document carefully the non-retaliatory reason for any adverse employment action.

17. PROHIBITION OF DISCRIMINATION IN THE WORKPLACE

17.1. Overview of U.S. Antidiscrimination Laws

Federal and state laws in the U.S. protect employees from unlawful discrimination in hiring, evaluating, discipline or termination and any terms and conditions of employment. Accordingly, employers in the U.S. may not take any job action against an employee based on the employee's age, race, gender identity, sexual orientation, disability, national origin, religion, military status, pregnancy, marital status or any other protected category. Federal laws prohibiting employment discrimination include, but are not limited to:

- Title VII of the Civil Rights Act of 1964 (Title VII).
- Americans with Disabilities Act (ADA).
- Rehabilitation Act of 1973.
- Age Discrimination in Employment Act (ADEA).
- Older Workers Benefit Protection Act.
- Equal Pay Act (EPA).
- Pregnancy Discrimination Act (PDA).
- Civil Rights Act of 1866 (section 1981).
- Genetic Information Nondiscrimination Act of 2008 (GINA).
- Uniformed Services Employment and Reemployment Rights Act of 1994 (USERRA).

The U.S. EEOC is responsible for enforcing federal laws that make it illegal to discriminate against a job applicant or an employee because of the person's race, color, religion, sex (including pregnancy), gender identity, sexual orientation, national origin, age (40 or older), disability or genetic information. The EEOC enforces Title VII, the PDA, the EPA, the ADEA, the ADA and the GINA. The EEOC also enforces laws that prohibit an employer from taking any adverse action (retaliation) against any employees who complain about discrimination, file a charge of discrimination, or participate in an employment discrimination investigation or lawsuit.

An applicant, employee or former employee who believes he or she has been discriminated against has the right to protest the alleged unlawful action by filing a charge with the EEOC within 180 days of the alleged discriminatory activity, or 300 days if there is an equivalent state law and a state agency enforcing that law. The EEOC will investigate the charge to determine whether it has any merit. The EEOC will then send a notice to the charging party in which it concludes that the claim has no merit or there is a probable cause of discrimination. If the EEOC includes no merit, the claimant has ninety days from receipt of the EEOC's notice in which to file a civil suit in a court of law. The EEOC can also bring private lawsuits against employers.

17.2. Age Discrimination

17.2.1. Overview

The ADEA, as well as most state and many local laws, protect employees of age 40 and over from employment discrimination based on their age. These laws generally apply to employers who employ twenty or more persons in each of twenty consecutive calendar weeks of the current or preceding year.

The ADEA prohibits covered employers in the U.S. from: (i) failing or refusing to hire, discharge or otherwise discriminate against any individual on the basis of the person's age; (ii) using employment advertisements that discriminate or in any way indicate a preference based on age; (iii) ceasing to contribute or accrue retirement benefits or reduce the rate of contribution or accrual under a retirement plan based on age; (iv) segregating, limiting or otherwise classifying employees in a way that adversely affects them due to age; or (v) retaliating against any person who has exercised rights under the ADEA.

17.2.2. Preemployment Process

An employer may not ask about an applicant's age or date of birth at any time during the preemployment process. Such questions are impermissible and can later serve as evidence in an age discrimination claim. An employer may ask whether an employee is over 18 years old and is eligible to work, but should not ask any questions which require a more specific answer, such as the applicant's birthday or what years the applicant attended high school.

17.2.3. Remedies

A successful ADEA claim may result in awards against the company for back pay, including the value of lost benefits, reinstatement, front pay, liquidated damages, and attorneys' fees and costs.

17.3. Race Discrimination

17.3.1. Overview

Title VII and section 1981, as well as most state and local laws, prohibit race discrimination. Title VII prohibits all forms of racial discrimination, including racial harassment, adverse employment actions based on race, as well as discrimination based on a facially neutral policy that has an adverse impact on a certain race. All employment decisions must be based on legitimate nondiscriminatory business reasons and not because of an individual's race.

17.3.2. Remedies

Under Title VII, successful plaintiffs can be awarded compensatory and punitive damages if the employer engaged in intentional discrimination with malice or reckless indifference to the federally protected rights of an aggrieved individual. Compensatory and punitive damages under Title VII are capped according to the size of the employer, but there is no cap to the amount of attorney's fees that can be awarded to a successful litigant.

Claims under section 1981 may also be tried before a jury and a claimant may recover compensatory damages, along with punitive damages and attorneys' fees. Section 1981, however, does not have a cap on recoverable damages.

17.4. Sex Discrimination/Sexual Harassment

17.4.1. Overview

Title VII, as well as most state and local laws, specifically prohibits any employment practice that discriminates against applicants or employees on the basis of sex. Title VII prohibits sex-based discrimination in all terms and conditions of employment, including: hiring, promotions, compensation, benefits and discipline. The Federal EPA also prohibits discrimination on the basis of sex and requires equal wages be paid for equal work on jobs that require equal skill, effort and responsibility performed under similar working conditions.

17.4.2. Remedies

Title VII allows individuals alleging intentional sex discrimination to recover both compensatory and punitive damages capped according to the size of the employer.

Title VII plaintiffs are also entitled to a trial by jury in addition to back pay, reinstatement, front pay and attorneys' fees.

17.4.3. Sexual Harassment

The EEOC defines unlawful sexual harassment in the U.S. by employers or their representatives as: "unwelcome sexual advances, requests for sexual favors, and other verbal and physical conduct of a sexual nature when: (i) submission to such conduct is made either explicitly or implicitly a term or condition of an individual's employment; (ii) submission to or rejection of such conduct by an individual is used as a basis for employment decisions affecting such individual; or (iii) such conduct has a purpose or effect of unreasonably interfering with an individual's performance or creating an intimidating, hostile or offensive working environment."

The two most serious types of sexual harassment are: (i) "quid pro quo" harassment; and (ii) "hostile work environment" harassment. In the EEOC's sexual harassment definition above, (i) and (ii) describe quid pro quo harassment while (iii) describes hostile work environment harassment.

In the U.S., employers can be held legally responsible for the actions of managers or supervisors who sexually harass employees if the supervisor's harassment results in a "tangible employment action," such as a significant change in employment status, including hiring, firing, failing to promote, reassignment of significantly different responsibilities or a decision causing a significant change in benefits.

Employers in the U.S. can also be held liable for sexual harassment by non-supervisors, coworkers, customers, vendors, or independent contractors if the employer "knew or should have known" of the harassment, but failed to take corrective action.

17.4.4. Same-Sex Harassment

"Same-sex" harassment claims can also be brought under Title VII. A plaintiff does not need to prove the alleged unlawful event was motivated by a sexual desire. Rather, a plaintiff must only demonstrate that the behavior was motivated by *gender* and it was so severe and pervasive that it would be offensive to a reasonable person in that context. In Bostock v. Clayton County, Georgia, 140 S. Ct. 1731 (2020), the U.S. Supreme Court confirmed that the protections of Title extends to individuals who are discriminated against in the workplace based on their sexual orientation or gender identity.

17.4.5. Sexual Harassment and Restrictive Covenants

The Speak Out Act renders unenforceable non-disclosure agreements and nondisparagement agreements entered into prior to a disputed claim of sexual harassment and/or sexual assault made by any victim who is a current, former, or prospective employee or even an independent contractor.

17.5. Disability (Handicap) Discrimination

The ADA, and most state and local laws, prohibits discrimination by an employer against a qualified individual with a disability who, with or without a reasonable accommodation, can perform the essential functions of their job.

The provisions of the ADA apply to job application procedures, hiring, promotion, compensation, training, discipline and other terms, conditions and privileges of employment. The ADA applies to employers in the private sector with fifteen or more employees.

An applicant or employee is considered disabled under the ADA if: (i) the person has a physical or mental impairment that substantially limits one or more major life activities; (ii) the person has a record or history of such an impairment; or (iii) the person is regarded by the employer as having such an impairment.

The Americans with Disabilities Amendment Act (ADAAA) modified the key phrase "major life activity" and the protections of the ADA now cover bodily and all major functions including, but not limited to: the immune system, normal cell growth, adjusted bowel, bladder, neurological, brain, respiratory, circulatory, endocrine and reproductive functions. Some of the other major life activities covered under the Act are sleeping, thinking, concentrating and communicating. Under, the ADAAA the condition need only limit one major life activity to constitute a disability

The ADAAA also expanded the "regarded as" protections by covering an employer's supposed perception of mental or physical impairment, even if it is not actually considered a disability, as grounds for discrimination. For example, a five-pound lifting limit that may not actually be a disability can still be the basis of a "regarded as" claim.

The ADAAA also expanded the ADA coverage to include individuals with episodic impairments or conditions in remission if the impairment substantially limits activity in the impairment's active state.

Finally, the ADA also prohibits employers from discriminating against employees who have a relationship with someone who is disabled, but it does not require reasonable accommodations for such employees.

17.5.1. Reasonable Accommodation

Of greatest significance, the ADA requires all covered employers to provide "reasonable accommodation" to an employee with a disability to enable the employee to continue to work and perform the essential functions of his or her job.

A "reasonable accommodation" may include, but is not limited to: (i) making existing facilities accessible to disabled individuals; (ii) restructuring nonessential job functions; (iii) job reassignment; (iv) modifying work schedules, such as providing part-time positions; (v) modifying existing equipment or acquiring new equipment; (vi) providing qualified readers, interpreters or assistants; and (vii) permitting unpaid leave.

In determining whether a "reasonable accommodation" is necessary or feasible, the employer should always involve the employee to help identify potential accommodations. An employer in the U.S., however, is not required to provide every accommodation requested by the disabled employee, or the best accommodation available. Rather, the accommodation must only be adequate to meet the job-related needs of the employee. The employer should document all efforts to accommodate an employee. If an employer fails to offer a reasonable accommodation, the employer could be subject to liability under the ADA, unless the employer can prove that the requested accommodation would constitute an undue hardship or would pose a direct threat to the health and safety of the individual, regardless of the accommodation.

An employer is not required, however, to provide an employee with an accommodation to perform his or her job which could cause an "undue hardship." An undue hardship arises when the accommodation would cause significant difficulty to implement, too expensive or fundamentally change the nature or operation of the business or service.

To determine whether an accommodation would be an "undue hardship," the following factors may be considered by the employer: (i) cost of the accommodation; (ii) financial resources of the accommodating employer; (iii) impact of the accommodation on business operations; (iv) number of persons affected by the accommodation; and (v) impact of the accommodation on coworkers.

17.5.2. Preemployment Inquiries

The ADA prohibits employers from asking an applicant whether he or she has a disability and/or the nature of the disability that may prohibit him or her from performing the job duties or whether they have ever been hospitalized or other health-related questions. The ADA also prohibits the use of "pre-offer" medical examinations and other selection criteria.

17.5.3. Accommodating Workplace Injury

Certain provisions of the ADA overlap with state worker compensation statutes. For example, if an employee is injured at work and is unable to return to his or her regular job, an employer may be required to create or modify a lighter workload program for the employee. The purpose of that type of accommodation would be to allow the injured employee to return to work sooner by offering work within the employee's permitted temporary restrictions.

17.5.4. Remedies

Remedies available under the ADA are the same as those under Title VII. If a plaintiff is successful, he or she is entitled to reinstatement or front pay, back pay, attorneys' fees and costs, but also limited compensatory and punitive damages.

17.6. National Origin Discrimination

Title VII prohibits discrimination based on national origin, as do many state and local laws. Under Title VII, national origin has been broadly interpreted to mean the country from which an applicant or employee, or his forebears came. In its interpretation of national origin discrimination, the EEOC also includes discrimination based on physical, cultural or linguistic characteristics of particular ethnic groups.

17.6.1. Remedies

If a plaintiff is successful, he or she is entitled to reinstatement or front pay, back pay, attorneys' fees and costs, and also limited compensatory and punitive damages.

17.7. Religious Discrimination

Title VII, as well as most state and some local laws, prohibits discrimination based on an applicant's religious beliefs. Employers must make reasonable accommodations for employees' religious needs, unless an accommodation would create an undue hardship for the employer's business. An employee must notify the employer of his or her need for a religious accommodation. An employer does not have to violate the seniority rights in a collective bargaining agreement in order to accommodate the religious beliefs of an employee. An employer should always seek suggestions from the employee regarding the best way to accommodate the employee's religious beliefs.

17.7.1. Remedies

If a plaintiff is successful, he or she is entitled to reinstatement or front pay, back pay, attorneys' fees and costs, and also limited compensatory and punitive damages.

17.8. Military Status Discrimination

Employers may not discriminate against employees on the basis of their military status. The USERRA of 1994 regulates leave for active and inactive duty and prohibits discrimination based on military status. Many state and local laws also prohibit discrimination based on military status.

17.9. Pregnancy Discrimination

The PDA prohibits a company from discriminating against an employee on the basis of pregnancy, childbirth, or any other pregnancy-related conditions. Federal and most state laws require that a company treat women affected by pregnancy-related conditions the same as all other applicants and employees with regard to their ability or inability to work and perform certain job-related functions. Importantly, a company may not disqualify pregnant employees from its medical benefits program, disability program, health insurance or sick leave plans. Rather, pregnancy should be treated the same as any other temporary disability.

Several courts in the U.S. also found it unlawful to discriminate against a woman because she has secured or refused to secure an abortion. On June 24, 2022, the US Supreme Court decided the case of *Dobbs v. Jackson Women's Health Organization,* No. 19-1392, 597 U.S. (2022) in which it held that the US Constitution does not protect a woman's right to an abortion. In overruling *Roe v. Wade*, the Court held that abortion is a matter/issue to be decided and regulated by local state law and state legislative bodies. As a result, several states promptly enacted/implemented laws greatly restricting or eliminating a woman's right to an abortion in a particular state. Some such states also imposed criminal and civil penalties on health care providers who perform abortions. Other states, most notably California, Illinois, New York, and Massachusetts, still protect a woman's right to have an abortion. In view of this decision, some large private employers in the U.S. are now considering/evaluating policies which may give employees paid time off to travel to other states to have an abortion.

The FLSA also requires employers to provide for one year following the birth of a child (i) reasonable (unpaid) break time for nursing mothers to express breast milk; and (ii) a private, secure space that may be used to express breast milk. Additionally, the Providing Urgent Maternal Protections for Nursing Mothers Act (PUMP Act) expands protections for breastfeeding parents previously provided by the Affordable Care Act of 2010 and employer obligations under the FLSA. The main updates under the PUMP Act include: (i) protections for employees who were not previously covered, particularly salaried employees; (ii) time spent expressing breast milk must be considered hours worked if the employee is also working; and (iii) the period of accommodations is extended from one year to two years.

Under the Pregnant Workers Fairness Act (PWFA), employers with fifteen or more employees are required to provide reasonable accommodations to job applicants and employees with conditions related to pregnancy or childbirth as well as prevents discrimination based on the need for a pregnancy-related accommodation. The PWFA mirrors the ADA's employee protections, but on a temporary basis, and is enforced by the EEOC, which provides guidance and examples of reasonable accommodations, including light-duty assignments, more frequent rest or bathroom breaks, ergonomic accommodations, etc. Employers will be subject to liability under the PWFA if they (i) do not make reasonable accommodations for an employee, unless they can demonstrate implementing the accommodation "would impose an undue hardship on the operation of the business;" (ii) require an employee accept an accommodation other than any reasonable accommodation arrived at through the interactive process; (iii) "deny employment opportunities if the denial is based upon the need of the employer to make reasonable accommodation; (iv) require an employee to take leave if another reasonable accommodation can be provided; or (v) "take adverse action in terms, conditions, or privileges of employment against a qualified employee on account of the employee requesting or using a reasonable accommodation."

17.10. Marital Status Discrimination

Marital status is not a protected status under federal law; some state and local laws protect employees from marital status discrimination.

17.11. Sexual Orientation/Gender Identity Discrimination

Title VII does not specifically prohibit discrimination based on sexual orientation. However, in its opinion for a trio of linked cases,[15] the U.S.

15. *Zarda v. Altitude Express, Inc.*, 883 F.3d 100, (2d Cir. 2018); *Bostock v. Clayton Cnty., Georgia*, 140 S. Ct. 1731, 207 L. Ed. 2d 218 (2020); *Equal Emp. Opportunity Comm'n v. R.G. &. G.R. Harris Funeral Homes, Inc.*, 884 F.3d 560 (6th Cir. 2018).

Supreme Court has held that Title VII prohibits employment practices that discriminate against applicants or employees on the basis of sexual orientation or gender identity, including transgender status.

17.12. Retaliation

The ADA, ADEA, Title VII and most state and local laws prohibit retaliation against employees engaging in any protected activities such as filing an administrative charge of discrimination, making a complaint of discrimination, and participating in an investigation of alleged discrimination. An adverse employment action which may constitute retaliation may include a post-employment action such as a negative reference. Employers should provide neutral job references when responding to inquiries about former employees.

Importantly, an employee does not have to be a member of a protected class in order to allege retaliation under Title VII. A worker who was fired for assisting with a coworker's claim of discrimination could have a claim for retaliation.

18. SMOKING IN THE WORKPLACE

Many employers in the U.S. now prohibit smoking in the workplace. Many states and municipalities also prohibit smoking in enclosed public places, including workplaces, except for clearly designated and posted smoking areas. Some of these states laws provide exemptions for certain premises such as bars, casinos and private clubs.

Although smoking is not a protected status under any federal law, in some states employers are prohibited from discriminating against employees on the basis of lawful tobacco use outside of the workplace or during working hours, including discrimination in hiring, termination, compensation, benefits and other terms and conditions of employment.

19. USE OF DRUGS AND ALCOHOL IN THE WORKPLACE

As a general rule, employers in the U.S. have the right to refuse to hire individuals who use illegal drugs and to establish rules that prohibit employees from possessing, using or selling illegal drugs or alcohol in the workplace. Employers may also investigate alleged drug and alcohol use by current employees at work and discipline employees who violate the employer's drug and alcohol policy.

Despite these general rules, the ADA may protect a "qualified" alcoholic who can meet the definition of "disability." The ADA may also protect a recovered drug addict who is no longer engaging in the illegal use of drugs. If covered by the ADA, the employee may be entitled to reasonable accommodations, such as a temporary leave to attend treatment programs. The ADA does not protect an individual who currently engages in the illegal use of drugs.

Despite the above, the ADA specifically allows employers to require an employee who is an alcoholic or who engages in the illegal use of drugs to meet the same standards of performance and behavior as other employees. Poor job performance or unsatisfactory behavior—such as absenteeism, tardiness, insubordination, or on-the-job accidents—is never protected behavior if all employees are treated the same.

Many private employers in the U.S. also require applicants or current employees be tested for drug and alcohol abuse. Employees may be terminated and applicants may be rejected if they test positive for illegal drugs or alcohol. Tests for illegal drugs usually may be given to prospective employees before a conditional offer of employment. Drug testing programs, however, are subject to state laws and regulations. For example, some states will allow an employer to test employees only under particular circumstances, such as when there is "reasonable suspicion" that an employee is under the influence of drugs or alcohol.

20. AIDS AND HIV

It is a violation of federal, state and local laws in the U.S. to discriminate against individuals with Human Immunodeficiency Virus (HIV) and the Acquired Immune Deficiency Syndrome (AIDS).

Individuals who are subject to adverse employment decisions simply because they have HIV or AIDS or because they "are regarded as" having HIV or AIDS may file a disability discrimination claim under the ADA or state or local law. Additionally, any such individuals claiming they have been subject to discrimination may also bring actions for defamation, invasion of privacy or violation of state or local AIDS confidentiality laws.

21. DRESS AND GROOMING REQUIREMENTS

Employers in the U.S. have legitimate and legally recognized interests in implementing a dress code or other grooming standard for the workplace. Many employers want to restrict employees from wearing distracting, offensive or otherwise inappropriate attire. Employers also want their employees to have good grooming habits. Dress codes can ensure the safety of all workers by prohibiting grooming habits or clothing that present safety, health, or hygiene risks. Concerns over the company's outward appearance to the public, however, generally do not apply to manufacturing and other nonpublic settings where the employees have little to no contact with customers. As a result, some employers have adopted more relaxed dress codes in manufacturing and technology business to improve morale and increase retention for nonpublic workplaces.

Employers may implement a reasonable dress code policy for employees during their working hours which provides clear descriptions of acceptable attire. The written dress code should provide assistance to managers and help avoid any misunderstandings about what is or is not appropriate. Employers should also train managers and supervisors on how to apply the dress code policy in a consistent, nondiscriminatory manner. Dress codes which restrict employees' rights to wear certain articles of religious or ethnic clothing can result in religious-based discrimination claims. Dress codes that impose more stringent rules on women can also give rise to sex discrimination claims.

Many dress codes are implemented to ensure safety in the workplace, and it is common for manufacturing companies to have rules prohibiting long loose hair or loose clothing. These types of rules will typically be upheld by courts as a lawful safety precaution. Employers should always explain the reasons a particular dress code or grooming standards help promote a company image or employee safety. However, some states impose additional restrictions on grooming policies. For example, New York prohibits discrimination based on hair texture or protective hairstyles as race-based discrimination.

Employers who require mandatory uniforms or safety or associated protective gear may be required to pay for the costs of such equipment, including maintenance, as well as pay for the time employees spend putting on and taking off such clothing or gear.

22. PRIVACY, TECHNOLOGY AND TRANSFER OF PERSONAL DATA

22.1. Privacy Rights of Employees

The explosion of personal technology and personalized access to the Internet in the form of social networking sites creates a number of dilemmas for employers seeking to keep their employees productive at work without instituting draconian policies regarding personal and private activity in the workplace.

Employers today have the ability to collect unprecedented amounts of information about employees, including information from nonwork-related activities. In some cases, employers may be tempted to monitor their employees on social networking sites, in their e-mail transmissions, and through the use of smartphones/PDAs issued by the company. Employers often seek to use this information in hiring and promotion decisions. Overlaying these efforts is an increasingly complex web of local, state and federal statutes and regulations promoting employee privacy, as well as international standards that may apply for companies with overseas operations. Employers must factor all of this into consideration before implementing any type of policies or actions that implicate an employee's privacy concerns.

22.1.1. Employee Monitoring

Employers traditionally faced relatively few limitations regarding the monitoring of employee's use of e-mail, Internet, instant messaging, company telephones, and other company systems, particularly if employees are informed of the types of monitoring that the company intends to undertake. Although this is generally still the situation, recent cases indicate that the legal landscape may be shifting and that courts are becoming more concerned about the privacy rights of employees. This is seen especially with regard to the monitoring of private e-mail accounts, private social media accounts, and other similar non-company applications (even if used on company computers or other company property).

Employee monitoring is not governed by one specific legal regime; rather, certain federal and state laws regarding wiretapping and intercepting of communications should be considered along with tort and constitutional considerations. The general legal framework as it relates to employee monitoring, as well as a brief discussion of recent case law, is set out below.

22.2. Federal: The Electronic Communications Privacy Act

Employee monitoring (e.g., monitoring of employee e-mail, Internet, instant messaging and telephone use) raises issues under a number of federal statutes, perhaps most notably under two provisions of federal wiretapping statutes—the Electronic Communications Privacy Act (ECPA), and the Stored Communications Act (SCA). The application of these laws merits careful consideration for any employer wishing to conduct employee monitoring. Very generally, a company should be able to conduct most employee monitoring if it obtains consent from one of the parties to such monitoring (e.g., the employee) or if it qualifies for other exceptions. Sufficient consent for these purposes can often be obtained through acceptance of computer use policies that expressly state that the company may monitor employee communications and activities on company systems and equipment.

At a high level, the requirements of the ECPA apply to the "interception" of "electronic communications." There is little case law that addresses the issue of whether employer monitoring of e-mail, web usage, and similar types of communications constitutes an "interception" under the ECPA. However, the First Circuit held that a company that collected information about web usage, including personally identifiable information, did intercept this data within the meaning of the Act. Assuming a company's monitoring activities would involve interceptions for purposes of the ECPA, two exceptions under the statute generally permit such monitoring. First, under the "provider exception," an employee of a provider of electronic communications services may "intercept, disclose, or use that communication in the normal course of his employment while engaged in any activity which is a necessary incident to the rendition of his service or to the protection of the rights or property of the provider of that service . . . "[16] To the extent a company qualifies for this exception, the company can monitor electronic communications to promote quality control, prevent loss of trade secrets, investigate employees suspected of wrongdoing, or deter personal use of company property. Even if the provider exception were found to be inapplicable in a particular case, companies can generally review employee communications and Internet use by obtaining express or implied employee consent. Second, as explained above, under the consent exception, an employer may intercept electronic communications if the prior consent of one of the parties to the communication has been obtained, and such consent generally may be obtained through acceptance of a company policy that expressly states that communications may be subject to monitoring.

22.3. Federal: The SCA

The SCA makes it unlawful to "intentionally access without authorization a facility through which an electronic communication service is provided" or to "intentionally exceed an authorization to access [a] facility." This statute is generally applicable to, among other things, e-mail communications that

16. ECPA, 18 U.S.C. §2511(2)(a).

have been received, and to voicemail messages. Courts typically find that an employer has the authority to review its own systems and equipment and is, thus, not in breach of the SCA, and there are exceptions to the prohibitions in the SCA that are comparable to the exceptions in the ECPA (e.g., a "provider exception" and a "consent" exception in section 2701(c)).

Recent trends suggest, however, that employers may no longer have rights to "unfettered" monitoring of employee activities. For example, a federal appellate court held that there were sufficient issues of material fact to deny an employer's motion to dismiss its employee's SCA claim for allegedly using passwords stored on the employee's work computer to access the employee's Twitter and Facebook accounts without her permission.

As a result, to the extent that an employer permits employees (either explicitly or tacitly) to maintain personal e-mail accounts, instant messaging services, or other personal applications (and the employer seeks to review such information), courts may be more sympathetic to claims that an employer's review constitutes invasion of privacy. Companies most likely can reduce the risk of success of such claims by prohibiting personal use of such applications or, perhaps more realistically, obtaining consents that explicitly state that any messages created via such applications will be subject to review if created on company systems or property.

22.4. State Wiretapping Laws

In addition to the ECPA and the SCA, many states also have wiretapping statutes. Like the ECPA and SCA, such statutes often are satisfied if one party to the communication consents to the monitoring. A few states, however, have two-party consent requirements that may be relevant to employee monitoring activities, which means that companies could in principle be required to obtain the consent of both parties to a communication before monitoring such communication. As companies may have difficulty obtaining the consent of both parties to e-mail, instant messaging or other types of messages that may be subject to monitoring, they should examine carefully the state laws in the relevant jurisdictions before engaging in such monitoring activities. Companies may also wish to consider taking affirmative steps to address the potential regulatory risks triggered by these statutes, such as: (i) updating employee e-mail "footers" to notify third-party recipients that the company may monitor e-mail; and/or (ii) seeking an affirmative expression of consent from employees to the acceptable use policy or other policy that notifies employees about the company's monitoring activities.

22.5. State Tort-Related Claims

In addition to statutory claims, employers could possibly face certain privacy-related tort claims as a result of their monitoring activities. Although this may change in an increasingly interconnected world of social networking, such claims generally should not prevail in most instances as long as the company has dispelled any reasonable expectation of privacy through company policies.

22.6. Federal and State Constitutional Issues

22.6.1. U.S. Constitution

The U.S. Constitution generally applies to a federal or state/local government agency's monitoring of employees, and it does not apply to monitoring conducted by private companies. Among other Constitutional provisions, the Fourth Amendment protects persons from "unreasonable searches and seizures" conducted by the government.

22.6.2. State Constitutional Provisions

In addition, some states such as California have established a right of privacy within the state constitution (*see Article 1, section 1 of the California Constitution*). To establish a privacy claim under this provision, the plaintiff must demonstrate: (i) a legally protected privacy interest; (ii) a reasonable expectation of privacy in the circumstances; and (iii) conduct by the defendant constituting a serious invasion of privacy. Again, employers can mitigate risks of claims under these types of provisions by taking steps to dispel any expectations of privacy by employees.

22.7. FCRA and Background Checks

22.7.1. Fair Credit Reporting Act

Many employers conduct background checks on prospective and current employees for evaluation and for various other reasons related to the employment relationship. When employers use third-party consumer reporting agencies to perform background checks, credit checks and investigations through use of a consumer report, employers need to be aware of and comply with the requirements of the FCRA or the Act.

To obtain a consumer report from a consumer reporting agency, an employer must sign a certification in compliance with 15 U.S.C. section 1681e of the FCRA, which requires the user/employer to certify its identity, the purposes for which the information is sought, and that the information will not be used for any other purposes. Employers generally must also provide a clear and conspicuous written notice to the applicant or employee of the employer's intent to procure a consumer report for employment purposes and obtain written authorization from the consumer to do so. If an employer intends to take any "adverse action" with respect to any consumer based on information in a consumer report, prior to taking such adverse action, it must give the applicant or employee: (i) a notice that includes a copy of the consumer report relied upon to make the decisions; and (ii) a description in writing of the rights of the applicant/employee under the FCRA, which may be found in the Federal Trade Commission's (FTC's) document "A Summary of Your Rights Under the Fair Credit Reporting Act."[17] If an employer does take adverse action based on information in a consumer report, the employer must provide: (i) notice of the adverse action to the consumer; (ii) information about the consumer reporting agency and the fact that the consumer reporting agency did not make the decision to take the adverse action; and (iii) notice of the consumer's right to obtain a free copy of the consumer report and dispute the accuracy or completeness of any such consumer report. "Adverse action" in relation to the employment relationship is defined broadly and includes "a denial of employment or any other decision for employment purposes that adversely affects any current or prospective employee." Employers who use "investigation reports" related to job applicants and employees (e.g., reports based on interviews with certain third parties related to the applicant's or employee's character, reputation or lifestyle) may be subject to additional obligations under the FCRA.

The FTC is charged with the enforcement of the FCRA. Under the FTC's authority, the FTC may conduct employer audits to determine whether an employer is using credit reporting agencies to conduct background checks and if so, whether the employer is acting in compliance with the FCRA's notice and other requirements. Failure to comply with the requirements of the FCRA may subject the employer to civil liability, and the FTC has the authority to seek civil penalties for noncompliance.

State law requirements relating to background checks and investigations may also apply. For example, some states may not allow questions about arrests or convictions beyond a certain point in the past. Other states may only allow consideration of specific information relevant to the position sought.

17. At https://www.consumer.ftc.gov/articles/pdf-0096-fair-credit-reporting-act.pdf.

22.8. FTC SECURE DISPOSAL RULE

In addition to the requirements of the FCRA, employers should also be aware of the FTC's secure disposal rule, which sets specific standards for the disposal of consumer information, which is broadly defined to include "any record about an individual, whether in paper, electronic, or other form, that is a consumer report or is derived from a consumer report." The law requires that "any person who maintains or otherwise possesses consumer information for a business purpose must properly dispose of such information by taking reasonable measures to protect against unauthorized access to or use of the information in connection with its disposal." Reasonable measures may include "implementing and monitoring of compliance with policies and procedures that require the destruction or erasure of electronic media containing consumer information so that the information cannot practicably be read or reconstructed." In addition, companies should conduct due diligence with respect to any party it engages to provide secure destruction of records and should monitor compliance to ensure that destruction is in accordance with the rule.

22.9. EMPLOYEE HEALTH CARE PRIVACY

22.9.1. Health Insurance Portability and Accountability Act

Employers that administer health plans for their employees (such as hospitals, health insurers and, in some cases, employers that offer employer-sponsored health plans) should also consider whether they are subject to the Health Insurance Portability and Accountability Act (HIPAA) of 1996. HIPAA contains standards with respect to the privacy and security of individually identifiable health information (collectively, the HIPAA Standards), and it is intended to provide individuals with notice regarding the use and disclosure of "protected health information" (PHI). PHI is information created or received by a covered entity relating to an individual's mental or physical health, health care or payment for health services. The HIPAA Standards also provide individuals the ability to request an accounting of disclosures of PHI, the ability to inspect or correct PHI and the ability to limit the purposes for which PHI may be used or disclosed without the express consent of the relevant individual. Violations of the HIPAA Standards as they apply to employers may lead to civil and/or criminal liability, even if such violations are made by the plan administrator, rather than the employer itself.

22.9.2. HITECH Amendments

In addition to the requirements discussed above, certain amendments to HIPAA also may affect employers and other parties that handle PHI. The Health Information Technology for Economic and Clinical Health Act, section 13001 of the American Recovery and Reinvestment Act, Public Law 111-005 (HITECH Ac or HITECH), established important amendments to HIPAA that include: (i) mandatory notification in the event of a security breach; and (ii) direct application of certain information security and other HIPAA provisions, including heightened penalty provisions, to an expanded range of organizations, such as: (a) business associates of covered entities (which previously only needed to adhere to agreements with such covered entities); and (b) application of breach notification obligations to vendors of personal health records (previously not covered by HIPAA).

Since the enactment of HITECH, the Department of Health and Human Services (HHS), through the HHS Office for Civil Rights, had engaged in considerable rulemaking activity and increased its enforcement of HIPAA's Privacy and Security Rules. Then, after a number of delays, HHS released on January 25, 2013, the final omnibus rules codifying and modifying many of these interim rules, including those regarding heightened penalties, breach notification and direct applicability to business associates (the "Final Rules"). The effective date of the Final Rules was March 26, 2013, and the covered entities and business associates were required to be in compliance with the new requirements by September 23, 2014.

These requirements have assumed increased importance under the HITECH Act due to enhanced consequences for HIPAA noncompliance (e.g., civil monetary penalties of up to USD 1,500,000.00 during a calendar year), as well as express enforcement authority for State Attorneys General, and additional authority for HHS to initiate criminal proceedings. In addition, with the increase in the number of high-profile security breaches, special focus on the breach requirements seems likely. There will likely be attention paid to how and if providers are subject to HIPAA (e.g., as business associates).

22.10. Information Security

22.10.1. State Information Security Law Requirements: Record Retention and Disposal

Many states have laws setting forth substantive security requirements applicable to the collection and handling of personal information. Such laws cover the secure handling of personal information, the secure disposal of such personal information and limitations on the uses a company may make of individuals' personal information, such as Social Security Numbers.

Many states have laws that require a company to maintain "reasonable" security measures for personal information. Generally, these statutes tend to be nonspecific, offering a company the ability to tailor its security measures to its business needs, and to the type of personal information at issue. For example, California law requires a business that owns or licenses personal information about a California residents, including employees or independent contractors, to "implement reasonable security procedures and practices appropriate to the nature of the personal information to protect the personal information from unauthorized or illegal access, destruction, use, modification, or disclosure."[18] Under the California Privacy Rights Act of 2020, an employer is further required to let its employees know what personal information they collect about them. Under the California Consumer Privacy Act of 2018 (CCPA), with similar acts adopted by other states, a business that discloses personal information to a third-party service provider must ensure, by way of contract, that such third party agrees to implement and maintain reasonable security practices designed to help protect personal data from unauthorized access, use, modification, disclosure or destruction.

Most states also have laws requiring the secure disposal of employee personal information. These laws tend to apply broadly to any information that identifies the individual. In California, the CCPA, for example, requires a business to take all reasonable steps to destroy or arrange for the destruction of records containing personal information that are no longer required to be retained by shredding, erasing or otherwise modifying the personal information in those records to make it unreadable or undecipherable. Under New York law, records must be shredded before disposal, personal information in the record must be destroyed, records should be modified to make the personal information unreadable or actions must be taken consistent with commonly accepted industry practices to ensure that no unauthorized person will have access to the personal information contained in the record.

22.10.2. Use of Social Security Numbers

In addition to requirements to safeguard and securely dispose of employee information, many states also have specific requirements relating to the use and protection of Social Security Numbers. Under Michigan law, for example, a company that possesses Social Security Numbers must create a

18. California Privacy Rights Act of 2020 § 1798.100(e).

privacy policy that ensures the confidentiality of Social Security Numbers, prohibits unlawful disclosure of Social Security Numbers, limits who has access to information or documents that contain Social Security Numbers, describes how to properly dispose of documents that contain Social Security Numbers and establishes penalties for violations of the privacy policy. The privacy policy must be published in an employee handbook, in a procedures manual, or otherwise made available electronically to employees.

In addition, Michigan, as well as many other states, has laws prohibiting certain uses of Social Security Numbers. Under Michigan law, for example, a business is prohibited from, among other things, using more than four sequential digits of a Social Security Number on any identification badge or card. Similarly, under California law, a company is prohibited from publicly posting or displaying an individual's Social Security Number. New York law, for example, also prohibits the printing of Social Security Numbers on employee identification materials, placing them in files with unrestricted access, or using them as identification numbers.

22.10.3. Recent Trends in State Information Security Laws

Recent changes in state laws indicate a trend toward more specific and more demanding state information security laws, including security breach notification statutes. Massachusetts, for example, enacted an information security law which is much stricter than most state laws on information security, and includes requirements for specific administrative, physical and technical safeguards, as opposed to more general requirements to maintain "reasonable" security.

The scope of entities covered by the law is broad in that it covers not only businesses within Massachusetts, but businesses residing outside of Massachusetts but who have employees or customers who reside in the state. This has potentially far-reaching consequences for a number of businesses and employers who will be required to comply with the law, even if located outside of Massachusetts. The law requires a covered entity to develop, implement, maintain and monitor a "comprehensive written information security program applicable to any records containing such personal information." The personal information subject to this regulation includes an individual's name in combination with the individual's Social Security Number, driver's license number, financial account number, or credit or debit card number. Whether the comprehensive written information security program (WISP) complies with the law is evaluated by taking into account such factors as the size, scope and type of business of the covered entity, the amount of resources available to the covered entity, the amount of data stored and the need for security and confidentiality of both consumer and employee information.

While the law seems to allow for some flexibility by allowing a covered entity to tailor the WISP to meet its own requirements, the law sets forth specific administrative, physical and technical safeguards that must be implemented for all covered entities. Covered entities that electronically store or transmit personal information also should include in their WISP the establishment and maintenance of a security system covering its computers, including any wireless system that meets minimum standards set out by the law to the extent technically feasible.

In Illinois, Illinois Biometric Information Privacy Act (BIPA) prohibits employers from implementing biometric-collection systems without first providing notice and obtaining individuals' consent.[19] It further provides that employers with biometric-collection systems may not "disclose, redisclose, or otherwise disseminate" biometric data to third parties without individuals' consent.[20] In February 2023, in the case of *Cothron v. White Castle System Inc.*, 2023 IL 128004, the Supreme Court of Illinois held that claims under BIPA accrue on each and every scan or collection of biometric data and further allowed so-called "scan damages," where a judge has the discretion to fashion an award that does not annihilate a defendants' businesses. This resulted in any person who uses a biometric device for any extended period without informed consent to collect millions individually, resulting in devastating damages for businesses in class actions.

22.10.4. Security Breach Notification Laws

Virtually all states have enacted statutes that require notification in the event of a security breach involving personal information. The security breach notification statutes apply to the personal information that a company holds, not only about its customers or consumers but also about its employees. While particular provisions on notice, reporting and penalties vary from state to state, most state security breach notification laws require that a business experiencing a security breach notify affected individuals if unencrypted personal information is disclosed or acquired in an unauthorized manner.

For purposes of the breach notification statutes, personal information is generally defined to include an individual's name or first initial and last name in combination with the individual's Social Security Number, driver's license or state identification card number, or the individual's financial account number or credit or debit card number in combination with any

19. 740 ILCS 14/1 § 15(b).
20. 740 ILCS 14/1 § 15(d).

required security code, access code or password that would permit access to the individual's financial account. Some state statutes have a broader definition of personal information, and a growing number of states are including health information with this definition. Virtually all state statutes apply only to unencrypted personal information, and the notification obligations generally do not apply when the information is encrypted.

22.10.5. US-EU Privacy Shield Certification Safe Harbor Privacy Framework

The implementation of the General Data Protection regulation (GDPR) in the European Union has required U.S. companies to change their data protection programs for the processing of personal data flowing from the European Union. In response to the more robust requirements imposed under the GDPR, U.S. companies may now participate in the Privacy Shield to conform with the new legal requirements.

The Privacy Shield program is administered by the U.S. Department of Commerce. Participating U.S. companies are required to self-certify that they are in compliance with applicable requirements and publicly commit to compliance with the Privacy Shield Principles and its supplements.

22.10.6. Social Media

Employers today face an emerging set of privacy issues related to social media and social networking. In an effort to promote brand identification and loyalty, to understand customer behavior and preferences, and to build deeper customer relations, marketing teams and business units are increasingly starting company "fan" pages on social media outlets such as Facebook, or MySpace, initiating company blogs through third-party sites such as Twitter, launching company blogs and online discussion groups on company sites, and otherwise entering into the arena of "new media" where users can publish their own content (User-Generated Content or UGC).

Employers should carefully assess the specifics of each new initiative and adopt a Social Media Policy that governs employee participation in such activities. One issue relates to ensuring that employees do not engage in practices that are misleading to customers and the public generally. For example, if employees do not identify their relationship with the company, effusive or other positive comments about company products or services may be considered an "unfair or deceptive" trade practice by the FTC. In 2009, the FTC issued its Guides for the Use of Endorsements and Testimonials in Advertising (the Guides) that describes the principles it expects companies to follow when allowing employee participation in these activities. In 2013, the FTC also released its first update to the Dot Com Disclosures Guide, which includes new guidance about disclosures that are relevant for social media marketing.

Another key issue relates to state legislative developments that prevent employers from requiring employees or prospective employees to provide passwords to social networking accounts. For example, Illinois has adopted a statutory prohibition against employers requesting or requiring any employee or prospective employee to provide any password or related account information in order to gain access to the individual's social networking account. The statute by its terms does not limit an employer's ability to promulgate lawful workplace policies and monitor usage of the employer's equipment, but is intended to guard employee privacy in personal, social networking communications. More than a dozen states have enacted similar laws, and similar measures have been introduced or are pending in nearly every other state.

Potential employee tort claims are another area that employers should consider. An employee may claim that he or she was subject to harassment by another employee in an online forum or raise a whistleblowing complaint. Employers will need to remain vigilant to address such issues in accordance with applicable company policies on harassment/discrimination, as well as handling whistleblower complaints (*see* sections 16 and 17).

In addition, employees that participate in social media and networking communications may have a greater risk of vulnerability to various data security threats, including viruses, malware and phishing attacks. Employers should increase awareness of computer use policies and procedures and confirm with information security personnel that company systems are properly protected from such data security threats. Among other concerns, if data security breaches occur, the company may have obligations to report the same to affected customers or other individuals under state or federal laws.

22.10.7. Bring Your Own Devices to Work

Employers are increasingly allowing employees to enable their own personal tablets, cell phones or other personal devices to access company systems (Bring Your Own Device or BYOD programs). These arrangements raise privacy concerns (i.e., employee concerns of privacy in their own devices) as well as security concerns related to increased loss of company data or other security issues related to access of company information and systems via personal devices. Employers need to be thoughtful when rolling out such programs and should take steps to address the unique privacy and security concerns raised by these programs.

22.11. Artificial Intelligence in the Workplace

More and more employers are utilizing AI in the workplace. Federal, state and local governments have started scrutinizing the use of AI tools by employers in response to the potential it will increase the possibility of bias or discrimination on the basis of protected activities or characteristics. While there is currently no existing federal law specifically targeted at AI use in the employment context, federal and state agencies responsible for enforcing employment statutes have begun to implement guidelines and regulations for employers to use when considering how to incorporate AI into employee decision-making.

In October 2022, the NLRB General Counsel published a memo addressing AI, cautioning employers against AI-empowered workplace surveillance, management tools, and other technologies that could unlawfully measure or base decisions upon protected activities or interfere with employees' ability to exercise their rights to engage in protected activities. It proposes a balancing test that would weigh an employer's business interest in using the technology against employee rights.

Additionally, The EEOC issued guidance for employers in May 2022 concerning the use of AI tools. For example, the EEOC guidance requires employers to provide reasonable accommodations to applicants who may be affected by automated decision-making tools due to their disabilities. As such, employers are responsible for vetting potential bias and discrimination against applicants with disabilities in AI-based hiring tools, even if a vendor provides the software. More recently, in January 2023, the EEOC issued a Draft Strategic Enforcement Plan that places employment discrimination in the use of AI technologies at the top of its strategic priorities list. In response, some state and local governments have begun prohibiting against the use of AI for automated employment decision-making tools in employment matters. For example, New York City passed a local law effective January 1, 2023, that prohibits employers from using AI-based employment decision tools to screen candidates or employees for employment decisions, unless the tool has been subject to a bias audit not more than one year prior to the use of the tool and the employer satisfies a series of burdensome notice requirements.

22.12. Checklist

- Employers should obtain employee consent to a Computer Use Policy that expressly states that the company may monitor employee communications and activities on company equipment.

- Employers should conduct a due diligence process to confirm that the company maintains reasonable information security measures to protect personal information from unauthorized access or use.
- Employers should adopt a WISP that addresses the requirements of state and federal laws for the protection of personal information and includes procedures for handling data security breaches or other privacy incidents.
- Employers should adopt a Social Media Policy to establish the rules for company initiatives related to Facebook, MySpace, Twitter or other online blogs or activities that allow employees to post UGC.
- Employers should not allow marketing or other business teams to launch initiatives into social media or other areas without consulting with Legal and/or Human Resources.
- Employers should not assume that information technology teams have developed sufficient information security policies and procedures to protect personal information without first checking on sufficiency under applicable privacy laws.
- Employers should not assume that a WISP and other privacy policies that were adopted more than a year ago are still current—privacy is one of the fastest developing areas of law.
- Employers should refer to their state and local government requirements with regard to the use of AI decision-making tools in the workplace and during the hiring process to prevent discrimination violations.

23. WORKPLACE INVESTIGATIONS FOR COMPLAINTS OF DISCRIMINATION, HARASSMENT, RETALIATION, FRAUD, THEFT AND WHISTLEBLOWING

23.1. Overview

In the U.S., a prompt and documented workplace investigation of employee complaints about discrimination, harassment, retaliation, fraud, theft, whistleblowing or any similar workplace occurrences provides protection and litigation defenses to an employer. Prompt identification and correction of any improper policies, procedures or behavior can also prevent litigation and provide the employer with the defense that it acted in good faith under the circumstances. That defense can help protect a company from legal liability, monetary damages and/or criminal liability. For example, under EEOC guidelines, an employer must conduct an investigation of any complaints of sexual or racial harassment and then take prompt remedial action to end the harassment.

Employers should keep in mind that a workplace investigation does not give a company the right to intrude into all areas of an employee's work or private life. Employers should not conduct searches of an employee's office, desk, locker, e-mail or voicemail without requesting and receiving the advice of counsel. In addition, employers should not record interviews or telephone calls, or capture an employee's e-mails or voicemails, without requesting and receiving the advice of counsel. State and federal laws may prohibit such conduct under electronic and wiretapping communications laws. Some investigations may also require written notice to and consent of the accused employee under state or federal background check laws. Employers should also exercise discretion when conducting a workplace investigation to avoid liability for suits relating to defamation or other torts by a falsely accused employee.

23.2. Checklist

- Carefully consider whether the investigation is best performed by a trained company representative, an impartial investigator, or an attorney under the attorney-client privilege, and determine to whom the investigator should report (HR, Legal, or the Board of Directors' Audit Committee).
- When conducting a workplace investigation, the investigator should determine the scope of materials to be reviewed, witnesses to be interviewed, privacy protections to be observed, and whether notice or consent is required under any applicable federal or state background check laws.
- Employers should make it clear that an investigator does not represent the employee or any witness. This is particularly important if the investigator is an attorney.
- Investigators should determine the sequence of interviews and establish the method for recording information from witnesses prior to conducting interviews.
- Investigators should not require nor promise confidentiality to any witnesses. A company is legally obligated to correct discriminatory behavior and may also be legally required to disclose the investigation to government entities, auditors, or in subsequent litigation. Employees may also be entitled to discuss the investigation under federal labor law. An employer can, however, require confidentiality of certain trade secret or proprietary information involved in the investigation.
- Employers should not use polygraph tests before seeking advice from counsel.
- After receiving notice of an employee complaint of discriminatory, retaliatory or unlawful conduct, companies should always issue a "litigation

hold" to retain, and not lose or destroy any documents and electronically stored information that can lead to admissible evidence related to the employee's claims or the employer's defenses. The retained information should include all information reviewed as part of the investigation process.

24. AFFIRMATIVE ACTION/NONDISCRIMINATION REQUIREMENTS

24.1. Overview

U.S. law requires employers who are federal government contractors and subcontractors to take affirmative steps to prohibit discrimination in recruiting, hiring, and employing any individuals based on their color, sex, religion, race, national origin, disability, and veteran status.

The laws which govern employment by federal contractors and subcontractors are Executive Order 11246, as amended (EO 11246), section 503 of the Rehabilitation Act of 1973, as amended (section 503), and the Vietnam Era Veteran's Readjustment Assistance Act of 1974, as amended (VEVRAA). These laws are administered by the Office of Federal Contract Compliance Programs (OFCCP).

Any company in the U.S. that enters any type of a contract with any federal government agency to provide supplies or services or to use or lease real or personal property may be deemed a federal contractor or subcontractor. "Services" include: utilities; construction; research; transportation; depository services; and insurance.

24.2. OFCCP Requirements for Federal Contractors

EO 11246 and section 503 require a business in the U.S. with a federal contract or subcontract of at least USD 10,000.00 to implement policies and procedures that require a contractor or subcontractor: (i) not to discriminate against any applicants or employees based on their protected status; (ii) take affirmative action to ensure applicants and employees are treated without regard to color, sex, religion, race, national origin, mental or physical disability and veteran status; and (iii) inform employees and applicants of the nondiscrimination policy. VEVRAA requires contractors to abide by these same provisions for protected veterans if they have non-aggregated contracts or subcontracts of at least USD 100,000.00.

24.3. VEVRAA

VEVRAA establishes the legal obligations of a federal contractor in the U.S. to recruit and hire certain types of veterans. VEVRAA was passed by Congress to prevent discrimination against returning Vietnam veterans seeking civilian employment.

VEVRAA prohibits federal contractors and subcontractors from discriminating against "protected" veterans in the hiring process and requires contractors to take affirmative action to ensure equal employment opportunities to veterans. Under section 503 and VEVRAA, federal contractors and subcontractors must take affirmative action to ensure that a certain percentage of all applicants hired for any positions are veterans protected under VEVRAA based on the national percentage of veterans in the civilian labor force.

Under the OFCCP's rules and regulations for section 503, contractors must also measure the total number of individuals with disabilities in their workforce and take affirmative action to hire and retain disabled veterans. Under VEVRAA, contractors must set an annual hiring benchmark for protected veterans, and update that benchmark annually according to the national percentage of veterans in the civilian workforce.

Under the OFCCP rules, the types of veterans who are considered "protected veterans" under VEVRAA include: (i) recently discharged veterans; (ii) disabled veterans; (iii) active duty wartime or campaign badge veterans; and (iv) Armed Forces service medal veterans. In addition, all contractors must ask individuals to voluntarily self-identify as individuals with disabilities and protected veterans at the pre-offer and post-offer stages. Moreover, contractors must periodically ask employees to voluntarily self-identify as individuals with disabilities throughout their employment. These new rules also require additional responsibilities of contractors and subcontractors when preparing and implementing Affirmative Action Programs (AAPs) (*see* section 24.4 below).

24.4. Establishing AAPs

Generally, businesses in the U.S. that are federal government contractors or subcontractors with fifty or more employees with a contract of USD 50,000.00 or more, or financial institutions who serve as a depository for government funds, are required under EO 11246 to prepare and implement a written AAP covering the employment of minorities and females in their workforce. Contractors with fifty or more employees and a contract of USD 50,000.00 or more are also required under section 503 to prepare and implement an AAP for individuals with disabilities. Contractors with fifty or more employees and non-aggregated contracts of USD 150,000.00 or more are required under VEVRAA to prepare and implement an AAP for protected veterans.

An AAP is a written document by which covered businesses describe the steps they will take to ensure equal employment opportunity for applicants and employees. As a general rule, an AAP for females and minorities must include the following quantitative analyzes: (i) an organizational profile; (ii) a job group analysis; (iii) incumbent employees in job groups; (iv) a determination of the availability of qualified women and minorities in the relevant labor market; (v) a comparison of incumbency to availability; (vi) job group placement goals; and (vii) an identification of problem areas.

Each site of a federal contractor, defined as a physically separate facility, must have its own separate AAP unless there are fewer than fifty employees at the site. In that case, the employees can be listed in the AAP of the enterprise where the human resources department or management is located.

AAPs developed and implemented under section 503 and VEVRAA also require: (i) the contractor's affirmative action policy statement; (ii) a review of personnel processes; (iii) a review of physical and mental job qualifications; (iv) a description how the contractor reasonably accommodates physical and mental limitations; (v) outreach and recruitment efforts; (vi) a summary of the internal and external dissemination of the contractor's affirmative action policy; (vii) actions taken to comply with audit and reporting requirements under section 503 and VEVRAA; (viii) the person assigned to prepare and implement the contractor's AAP; (ix) a summary of personnel training; and (x) data collection analyzes of applicants and hires.

If a contractor or subcontractor does not comply with the rules and regulations issued by the Secretary of Labor or the OFCCP, that contractor or subcontractor could face sanctions including: back pay and interest; cancelation or termination of the federal contracts; restrictions on the contractor receiving future government contracts; and enforcement proceedings brought before the Department of Justice or the EEOC.

25. RESOLUTION OF LABOR, DISCRIMINATION AND EMPLOYMENT DISPUTES: INTERNAL DISPUTE RESOLUTION, MEDIATION AND CONCILIATION, ARBITRATION, AND LITIGATION

Employment disputes are subject to a variety of resolution techniques. Because of the costs of court litigation and the unpredictability of outcomes of jury trials, employers often seek alternative ways to resolve disputes.

25.1. Internal Dispute Resolution Processes

Many employers in the U.S. maintain "open-door" dispute resolution policies, which encourage employees to raise workplace issues informally, and resolve problems directly with their supervisor or manager. Typically, these type of policies allow an employee to resolve an issue by going to successively higher levels of supervision up to senior management.

Informal dispute resolution processes are inexpensive, frequently effective, and can be an important factor in improving employee morale, productivity and overall corporate effectiveness. Such a process can resolve disputes early and make management aware of problems before any litigation. Open-door policies will not, however, by themselves, prevent an employee from filing a lawsuit or administrative complaint with a government agency.

Many companies in the U.S. also have some type of a formal "complaint" or "grievance" procedure involving multiple steps of review and requirements for participation. Most union contracts also have grievance or arbitration procedures which can act as alternatives to litigation and even preclude litigation.

Internal "complaint" procedures give employees the right to raise any issues of concern with management and have their issues "heard" by various levels of management within the company. In nonunion companies, the last step of a complaint procedure may be a senior management review, or a peer review panel consisting of employee and management representatives. The panel in some cases may have the authority to conduct an informal hearing and impose a resolution that is binding on both the company and the employee. Some companies have also implemented arbitration as a final step.

Companies typically have policies that prohibit retaliation against employees for filing complaints either internally or with government or law enforcement agencies or participating in any complaint process.

25.2. Mediation and Conciliation

Mediation is frequently used when a lawsuit is threatened or after the filing of a lawsuit. The EEOC and some other government agencies also use mediation as part of their administrative charge process. Some courts also require the parties to engage in mediation before proceeding to a trial. Mediators are normally selected by joint agreement of the parties or can be appointed by a court or agency. They have special training in dispute resolution and are often lawyers or former judges with a special expertise.

They do not determine liability or assess damages, but only seek to help the parties reach a mutually acceptable binding agreement to resolve the dispute.

The mediation process is considered confidential and statements that are made and information that is given as part of the mediation process is considered part of settlement discussions and cannot be used as evidence in a court proceeding. Mediation proceedings are usually not discussed by either party outside of the mediation setting.

The principal advantage of pre-litigation mediation is the resolution of complex disputes without the cost of time-consuming litigation. In addition, parties have control over the terms of a mediated agreement, as opposed to a court imposing a public remedy that neither side finds acceptable. Mediation decisions are non-precedential; that is, they do not have any effect on other cases or interpretations of the law. Parties can also present arguments in mediation that would not be admissible in court. In addition, because of their confidential nature, private mediation can avoid the threat of negative publicity that can occur during the litigation process. In addition, mediation is almost always faster than a trial.

Private mediation can still be expensive because the parties will incur mediation costs as well as costs of preparing and attending the mediation. Parties frequently learn facts in mediation; however, that will help them either resolve or settle a lawsuit later in the process. For example, it is not uncommon to learn the true motivations behind an employee's lawsuit or complaint during a mediation, which is frequently not evident from the complaint or a charge of discrimination.

25.3. Arbitration

In union settings, final and binding arbitration is generally the last step of a grievance procedure in a collective bargaining agreement.

Over the past several years, many nonunion private sector employers in the U.S. have also implemented policies requiring all employees to pursue any claims against the company by private arbitration rather than pursue their claims before a federal or state court or a jury. Many employers are also requiring new hire or current employees to sign agreements by which they waive their right to participate in a class or collective action even if their claim is subject to arbitration. In its 2018 decision, the U.S. Supreme Court decided in *Epic Systems Corp. v. Lewis*, that class and collective action waivers in employment arbitration agreements are lawful and may be enforced under the Federal Arbitration Act.

Although some states have attempted to limit an employer's ability to compel the private arbitration of employment dispute, the U.S. Supreme Court has continued to uphold private arbitration. On June 15, 2022, in the case of *Viking River Cruises v. Moriana,* the U.S. Supreme Court upheld the mandatory arbitration of private PAGA claims in the context of California law. The California Supreme Court had earlier held that PAGA claims could not be subject to mandatory arbitration.

A recent amendment to the Federal Arbitration Act will likely impact the viability of private arbitration. On March 3, 2022, President Biden singed into the law the Ending Enforced Arbitration of Sexual Assault and Sexual Harassment Act 2021 (the "Amendment"). Under the Amendment, prevents employers from enforcing mandatory pre-dispute arbitration agreements as well as agreements prohibiting participation in a joint, class or collective action in any forum, unless the employee alleging sexual harassment or sexual assault consents. Thus, individuals asserting sexual assault or sexual harassment claims under federal or state law may elect to pursue them in court. The law does not invalidate existing arbitration agreements. Rather, the Amendment gives employees the option to pursue such claims in court or in arbitration. Courts will decide whether the Amendment applies to a particular dispute. Arbitration takes place before a single arbitrator or a panel of arbitrators. The arbitrator, or arbitration panel, will normally have the authority to hear evidence and make a final decision as to liability, remedies and damages. Arbitrators in the nonunion setting have the power to award all remedies available to an employee under the appropriate federal or state law, including reinstatement with the former employer, back pay, front pay, compensatory damages, and, in some cases, even punitive damages. Arbitration decisions are binding and enforceable and are subject to limited review by the courts.

Some of the potential advantages of private arbitration are: (i) the parties may obtain more well-reasoned decisions when factual determinations are made by an arbitrator who is a subject matter expert rather than a jury comprised of laypersons; (ii) arbitration may result in more reasonably calculated damage awards and may be less costly and faster than court litigation; (iii) an arbitration agreement with an employee may prohibit the employee from joining in a class or collective action lawsuit; and (iv) arbitration is generally more confidential.

Some of the potential disadvantages of private arbitration are: (i) it is very difficult to overturn an arbitrator's award; (ii) in some cases, an employee can litigate claims at the same time before an arbitrator and in a court proceeding or before a government agency; (iii) some arbitrators may decide cases erroneously, which generally are very difficult to appeal or overturn and arbitrators are hesitant to grant dispositive motions; (iv) arbitration can sometimes be as expensive as litigation; and (v) litigants may still have the same posttrial remedies.

25.4. Litigation

Court (or government agency) litigation is generally considered the most costly and time-consuming form of dispute resolution in the U.S. because of its formality, the lengthy and involved pretrial discovery and deposition process, and the requirements placed on the parties before bringing a case to trial. Employment litigation occurs in state or federal courts (or in certain municipalities, before a municipal or city court), with significant burdens imposed on both parties to engage in discovery and development of evidence prior to trial, the production of evidence for trial, related trial submissions, the trial itself, and posttrial proceedings.

25.4.1. Single and Multi-plaintiff Litigation

The allegations of a lawsuit are typically based on either statute (i.e., the employer is alleged to have violated a particular statute) or common law (the employer is accused of violating some widely recognized and enforced obligation or a duty to the employee). Depending on the claim—the "cause of action"—the employer can assert statutory or common law defenses if the case ever goes to trial. In many employment cases, the company may be able to resolve the case prior to trial by procedural mechanisms known as motions "to dismiss" or "for summary judgment." By this process, the employer convinces the court that there is essentially no basis in law or fact to hold a trial. Employees may also move for summary judgment arguing that undisputed evidence establishes the employer's liability. More than 95% of the civil cases that are filed in the U.S. are settled or dismissed prior to a trial before a judge or jury.

25.4.2. Class Action Litigation

Class action litigation can be filed in state or federal courts. A class action judgment can bind current or former employees who are not participants in the lawsuit itself. Class action cases occur when there is a large group of employees who are affected by the same policy, or whose work conditions are sufficiently similar that a resolution of the claims of one or more individuals can be effectively applied to the entire group.

Class actions must be certified. This means that a court formally designates the class and describes its members and the scope of the representation. This typically occurs as a result of a motion filed by the representative plaintiffs. The defendant employer may object to the class certification, and courts may reject class certification petitions because the interests of the employees are too different from each other to be resolved in a single trial.

The requirements for a class action under most federal laws (which have been adopted by many state courts as well) are: (i) the class must be so numerous that individual lawsuits are impractical or would impose an undue burden on the court; (ii) the parties must have legal and factual similarities in their claims; (iii) the claims at issue must be typical of the class; (iv) the representative parties (the individuals who will actually be represented at the trial) must adequately protect the interest of the entire class; (v) common issues of fact and law predominate; (vi) individual differences and specific conflicts between class members and defendants must be minimal; and (vii) the class action is a superior means of resolving the disputes at issue as opposed to individually litigating each of the claims.

As discussed above in section 25.3, many employers have implemented arbitration agreements or policies which require employees to waive their right to litigate or arbitrate their claims in a class or collective action. The U.S. Supreme Court's decision in *Epic Systems Corp. v. Lewis* has made it clear that such waivers are enforceable (*see* above).

25.5. Fines, Penalties and Damages

Courts and arbitrators have the ability to impose a variety of remedies under both statutory and common law theories. Damages include compensation for pain, suffering and emotional distress, back wages for lost earnings, other economic losses, and compensation for embarrassment or humiliation suffered as a result of an employer's action. An employer can also face penalties such as front pay (compensation for lost wages going forward from trial if the court determines that the individual is unable to work as a result of the employer's action), statutory civil penalties, as well as attorney's fees under federal and state employment statutes.

Punitive damages may be the largest part of an adverse judgment if they are available. They are not awarded to compensate the plaintiff, but to punish or deter the employer from engaging in similar conduct in the future. Punitive damages are awarded only in certain circumstances; for example, where the employer has willfully violated a statute, or has acted in a particularly egregious or outrageous manner. Punitive damages are limited under some statutes.

26. EMPLOYER RECORDKEEPING, DATA PROTECTION AND EMPLOYEE ACCESS TO PERSONNEL FILES AND RECORDS

26.1. Overview

An employer must retain certain personnel records for specific periods of time under both federal and state laws.

26.2. Personnel Files

Federal laws generally require that personnel records, including applications, promotion and termination records, tests and similar records, must be maintained for one year.

Other record-keeping requirements include:

- The most recent EEO-1 record must be maintained at each separate company location for employers with 100 or more employees.
- Standard screening and hiring records must be maintained under both the ADEA and the Service Contract Act for a period of three years.
- Records relating to employee identification, payroll, certificates, collective bargaining agreements and other employment notices must be maintained by the employer for three years.
- Records relating to time cards, work schedules, rate tables and similar documentation must be maintained for a period of two years.
- ERISA plan records, including summary plan descriptions, annual reports and similar documentation relating to ERISA plans, must be maintained for six years.
- Tax records indicating employee identification, salary, payment dates and withholding taxes must be maintained for four years.
- Records relating to I-9 verification, including forms and other documentations, must be maintained from the later date of either three years from the hire date or one year following termination.
- Records relating to workplace health and safety, such as Form 300, must be maintained for five years.
- Records (including name and Social Security number of relevant employees) relating to blood-borne pathogens and exposures at the workplace must be maintained for the entire period the employee is employed, as well as thirty years following the cessation of employment.
- If the employer is a federal contractor, all personnel or employment records must be maintained for two years if the contractor employs 150 or more employees or for one year if the contractor employs less than 150

employees or does not have at least a USD 150,000.00 contract with the government.
- Records relating to requests for and granting of FMLA leave, including the length of the leave, as well as notices and copies of the FMLA policies and benefits, must be maintained for at least three years.

26.3. Confidentiality Rules

Employee personnel files and related information should be maintained in the strictest confidence. Absent written authorization from an employee, an employee's information should only be accessed by those with a valid need, unless an order of a court directs otherwise. All documents containing an employee's medical information must be maintained separately from the employee's personnel file.

26.4. Employee Access

State and local laws generally allow an employee to access his or her own personnel records and, in certain circumstances, to correct inaccuracies within the personnel record. While federal law does not require such access, an employer should always reference relevant state and local laws before denying an employee access to the employee's own personnel records.

27. REQUIRED NOTICES AND POSTINGS

27.1. Overview

Federal law and some state and local laws require most employers to place specified notices in the workplace where employees can easily view them. Employers may order required posters at www.dol.gov/compliance/topics/posters.htm. This site also helps employers determine which notices they must have depending on the industry and working conditions of the employee.

Below are some of the notices that must be posted by most employers under federal law and also some of the federal laws requiring notices:

- "Employee Rights under the Fair Labor Standards Act" (FLSA).
- "Job Safety and Health: It's the Law" (OSHA).
- "Employee Rights and Responsibilities under the Family and Medical Leave Act" (FMLA).
- "Equal Employment Opportunity is the Law."

- "Occupational Safety and Health Act" (OSHA).
- "Migrant and Seasonal Agriculture Worker Protection Act" (MSPA).
- "Employee Polygraph Protection Act" (EPPA).
- "Davis-Bacon and Related Acts" (DBRA).
- "McNamara-O'Hara service Contract Act" (SCA).
- "Walsh-Healey Public Contracts Act" (PCA).
- "The Uniformed Services Employment and Reemployment Rights Act" (USERRA).

www.ingramcontent.com/pod-product-compliance
Lightning Source LLC
Chambersburg PA
CBHW071352230926
51846CB00002B/530
9789403501895